Lost Blood

Lost Blood

Marco Abraham

ISBN 978-0-615-17247-7

First Edition 2007

Printed in the United States of America by Mennonite Press, Inc., Newton, KS

Published by Marco Abraham

Contact the author at:
MarcoAbraham@yahoo.com
www.MarcoAbraham.com

Production Credits:

Cover, Text Design and Production: Sandi Nelsen
Front Cover Photo is of an unknown child and is public domain as far as author can determine. Photographer unknown.
Back Cover Photo: Portrait Innovations

Library of Congress Control Number: 2007924854

Abraham, Marco, 1965 -
Lost Blood / by Marco Abraham. --1st ed.

THIS BOOK IS WRITTEN IN MEMORY OF THE SABRA AND SHATILA VICTIMS

SPECIFICALLY FOR ONE SPECIAL VICTIM
WHO RISES
ABOVE THEM ALL
THE TRUE ANGEL – THE TRUE HERO

A GIRL NAMED ROLA

CONTENTS

CHAPTER ONE

Life in the Sabra and Shatila Camps Before the Massacre

I was born at 5:45 p.m. on February 20th, 1965, in a small refugee camp called Shatila in Beirut, Lebanon. Shatila camp was built in the early fifties for the Palestinians who left their country, Palestine, after the Israeli occupation in their land in 1948. The houses in my camp are made from concrete except the roof, which is thin sheet metal. It is very loud in my house on the rainy days. I can hear every drop of rain on the roof. Shatila camp is connected to a smaller camp called Sabra—another small Palestinian refugee camp. They are connected by a single street called Elmograbi, which refers to a young lady suicide bomber who blew herself up in South Lebanon in 1978 against the Israeli Army. In my camp, there is one school called Al-Jaleel. I will go

to this same school from first grade through high school. There are two hospitals: Gaza and Akka. The population of my camp, Shatila, is around fifteen thousand, and I would say Sabra camp is estimated around thirteen thousand.

I grow up living through a very long and painful civil war. The war is between the PLO, the Palestinian Liberation Organization, which is under the leadership of Yasser Arafat on one side, and the Lebanese groups on the other. Growing up as a small boy is very painful; it is not a childhood at all. The streets are not safe and even toys can be explosive traps. We are warned by the PLO soldiers repeatedly not to touch anything on the streets, and especially anything that looks like a toy. We have to avoid playing at all for fear of losing limbs; I witness children being maimed or killed on the streets often.

Again, the civil war is a turning point in my childhood. I start to see the dead bodies multiply on the streets of the camp from the falling rockets, the people with fewer and fewer limbs. I was very young then, but I remember when this civil war started, in the early seventies. As I remember, my parents warned me not to leave the house, as they are worried for my safety. I stay home most of the time, just like every kid in the camp, but the precaution is a false safety. Everywhere in the tin-roofed camp is dangerous.

Either way death is waiting for us outside.

I live in a one-bedroom house with my mother, father, and seven of my brothers. Actually, it is not that bad—cozy almost. My brothers and I are very close; we are separated only by a little over a year between one another. My mom is a true survivor, as she holds the big family together. Even with very limited or no resources, as far as food and income. There are no jobs in the camps except small street shops. Bread, cigarettes and soft drinks are the main merchandise to be had.

There is one furniture store on the south end of the camp. This furniture store is owned by my best friend's family. My best friend Abud Alsalam and I are very close, as we go to the same school together throughout all our school years.

In the late seventies he began to drive his dad's old Nissan pickup that they used for furniture delivery. He and I used to steal the truck after Abud Alsalam's father was in bed. We would drive to a deserted field called Jalool Land, between Sabra and Shatila camps. Abud Alsalam is of medium build, about five feet eight inches with short black hair always combed straight back. His sharp big brown eyes betray the iron strength of his personality. The loyalty between us has no limit. Growing up we look out for each other, hardly leaving each others side; this has made us the best friends that we are today.

The open field is perfect for driving lessons, my friend took the time to teach me how to drive his stick shift truck. Not long after that I am the one to be spotted behind the wheel all the time.

We take little notice of the dead bodies on the side of the road on our joy rides as death had become part of our daily life. No one can keep up with the rising death toll, excess corpses litter the camp.

We see so many dead people that as we grow older we stop paying attention. The horrifying stench from the exposed bodies chokes in our throats, so strong we can taste it. But again we become used to this as well. There is no escape.

In the beginning it makes me sad to see the bodies of my friends and neighbors lying on the narrow streets of the camps, as I cannot help to remember how they had been such a short time ago.

My mind adjusts itself so that dealing with this environment becomes routine.

I ignore all of it.

In the meantime, I am still attending school. Every school day morning, the teacher calmly announces the one, two, or sometimes three newly killed students. This too becomes old news, making little impact.

Most days after school, Abud Alsalam and I go target shooting with a Russian-made AK-47 in an empty field called Asas field, not too far from the camp. We pack our backpacks with live ammo given to us by the friendly PLO soldiers. We select a target, usually a large pine tree.

At age 13 we enjoy the rush of using the semi-automatic weapon that shoots off thirty bullets in seconds.

The AK-47 is our toy, there are plenty of them—they are easily picked off of a dead body who obviously has no further use for it. I'm sure they do not mind.

When there is a cease-fire for a couple days between the PLO and the Christian Lebanese in Eastern Beirut, that is when fighting breaks out between the PLO factions, leaving behind more casualties. The action never stops, I am never bored.

One day we start to experience a new way of killing. People are minding their own business walking down the street and then fall dead instantly. In a single shot to the head, snipers from the East side of Beirut are a change of pace from the rockets we are used to.

The Christian Lebanese begin to use more advanced sniping weapons. When this begins, everyone walking on the street walks in zigzags trying not to give the snipers a clear shot.

For the next two months we avoid leaving home completely except for emergencies. Snipers are the only things that we can never grow used to. In my opinion, that is the scariest thing I have yet to experience.

One day some of my classmates and I are playing a soccer game in Jalool Land when suddenly the players begin falling to the ground one by one. We realize there are snipers targeting us, everyone runs for cover to the nearby Gaza hospital, about two hundred feet away, but only after six of the players lose their lives. As children, we do not know any better than to make such easy targets of ourselves. We stay at the hospital about ten hours, until two the next morning, for fear of snipers waiting for us. Sitting just inside the doors, we are scared, joking nervously and waiting for the right moment to escape. In the darkness of early morning we all make a dash for our homes, exhausted and starving by the time we arrive. I feel lucky to have survived this soccer game. Then again, I am living in one of the most dangerous places on the face of the earth.

My mother has waited and cried for me all night long sitting on the doorsteps, as she's heard about the six kids who had been shot dead on the soccer field. Not knowing if I am among the living or the dead, she runs towards me as I run down our street, embracing me on her knees while sobbing.

I am thirteen in the summer of 1978 when three of my friends and I have a crazy idea to take the forty-five minute walk to the

White Sand, the nearest beach. This area—and even the idea of leaving Shatila—is forbidden. None of us have ever ventured beyond the camp, hearing only stories of the coast. It is the worst idea in the history of bad ideas. The sweltering day with no air conditioning or fans to bring relief prompts the four of us to think five minutes in the water worth dying for. We walk about four miles toward the beach, careless and fearless as we joke in fun on the way. Finally arriving, we scale the high rocks and jump fully clothed into the beautiful clear blue water. For the next two hours we have a blast, the most fun we have had in our young lives and a definite change from our normal existence. We of course have not informed our parents of our trip, so we decide to head back, even though it is hard to leave the beach behind.

We are assuring each other of the need to come back often as we leave when an army green British-made Land Rover stops us. We are unsure of what militant group they belong to. Scared, we stand helplessly looking at each other waiting for the unknown. One soldier in particular who is seated next to the driver withdraws his handgun, aiming it an inch or two from my face. He asks calmly, "Where you boys from?"

Not knowing if there is a right answer to the question and seeing his hidden anger, I tell the truth and reply, "From Shatila Camp." With that said, the other five armed soldiers jump out of the vehicle as if my answer had hit the spot.

They start to beat us on every inch of our bodies. They punch and kick their boots into our faces as we lay on the ground. All of us are bruised, swollen and bleeding profusely from our mouths and noses from the ten minutes of continuous abuse. It would have lasted longer except for an old man passing by who came to the rescue. All he screams is “Leave them alone they are just kids!” This is enough to earn him a blow to the head with the bottom of an M-16 rifle. He falls to the ground from the single hit while the soldiers turn their attention back to us. They drag us together, pile us on top of each other and proceed to urinate on us as they laugh. They say as they leave, “Consider this a warning—Don’t ever come back here again.”

Standing up we laugh at our swollen disfigured selves, we think the whole experience is the funniest thing, as is the blood everywhere.

We feel lucky they did not shoot us. Once again I have cheated death.

The school is the first stop before we go to our homes. We take turns hosing each other off with water to at least rinse the blood and urine from our bodies. We agree not to tell anyone about our adventure, answering my mother’s questions when I got home with “I just got in a fight with some kids.” This is the end of the matter.

Life keeps on this way without a break, I survive on a day by day basis until the big day, June 6, 1982. It is the day the Israeli army moves into South Lebanon. The big invasion. Israel has one thing on their mind, to destroy the PLO and drive them out of Lebanon completely.

Israel has the most advanced army in this part of the world, powered by the best that technology has to offer. Tanks, fighter jets, ground troops and spy satellites give Israel an instant upper hand compared to the impoverished PLO, who are equipped with Russian-made weapons from the Second World War. Without tanks

or heavy artillery, the odds are, of course, in favor of the Israeli forces. Once they cross the border in the South, they befriend and receive aide from guerillas who oppose the PLO. With that much military power and internal help—despite the strong PLO resistance effort—it does not take the Israeli army long to reach and encompass Beirut. The city is being surrounded and weakened by the barrage of 960 tons of ammunition dropped mostly from F-16 jet fighters on one side, and rockets banned by international war laws on the other.

The Israeli army surrounded Beirut for almost three months, preventing food and medical supplies from entering the city to reach the hungry and injured civilian inhabitants. Even the water supply is cut.

The siege continues to put pressure on the PLO for a quick surrender and the bombing of Beirut never ceases even as the people perish. The mounting number of wounded have no aid, the people no food or water.

During this time, the F-16 fighters keep bombing the Sabra and Shatila camps all day, every day. The explosion from the rockets is a sound I am unfamiliar with. The power and volume of the impact and explosion are so intense that my ears bleed continually. The rockets themselves leave craters fifty feet in diameter. The increased distress makes me consider my former life as easy compared to this new reality. In addition to the craters, the dead body count on the streets increases dramatically—walking without stepping on the dead people is impossible.

In the middle of 1982 I am almost eighteen years old, even with all the carnage and action around it is the best year for me—it is the year I meet Rola. She is almost eighteen as well. We meet in a basement shelter where all the women, children and elderly hide from the Israeli airplane bombers. I meet Rola coincidently while visiting my mother in that same shelter. I notice she is helping all the people around her, cooking and serving in the dim candlelight. A slim five-foot-seven with black silky hair, long down the middle of her back, I can only describe her as drop-dead gorgeous. I watch her doing all the things in the shelter to comfort the petrified families; hand feeding the wounded and changing diapers.

She is the angel of this damned camp, I am smitten.

I cannot help but ask my mother who is this beautiful young girl. Smiling, she whispers, "She is beautiful, isn't she?"

I blush from my lack of experience in this kind of situation. To my surprise, in a loud voice my mother calls Rola from across the room. She says, "I want you to meet my son." Embarrassed and smiling, I can see the shyness in her eyes. She does not say a word to me, but asks my mom if she needs any help. At her negative reply Rola quickly walks away.

I whisper in my mom's ear, "Keep her close to you, I will come visit you more often."

My visiting habits go from once every three or four days to every day—three or four visits—for one reason, to watch Rola doing God's work. All during my time in the shelter, as she ministers to the people, our eyes rarely lose contact. My mother always seems to receive extra attention from Rola, my mother loves her like a daughter. Noticing my interest in Rola, my mom is pleased and comments that if this is the only way to keep me safe in the shelter, then so be it.

Between my visits I am still doing my thing, which is helping the wounded people on the streets by carrying or dragging them to Rola's shelter. Unfortunately, most of them die within hours from their severe wounds, but some are fortunate enough to show signs of improvement.

In the meantime I begin to notice that the portions of food in the shelter become smaller and smaller, almost down to nothing. On my last visit I have to ask my mom about the food situation. That is when she tells me they eat only one meager meal a day. I decide then that I have to do something more for these people.

I go to visit with my best friend Abud Alsalam at his house, he is sleeping when I arrive. My question for him is, "How could you sleep with all this bombing?"

"Well, If I am going to die, I will die here in my bed."

I tell him that no one is dying today, but that a lot of the shelter people will if we do not do something to help them.

"What shelter people?" is his reply.

I explain about what is happening where my mother is staying, he reminds me that there is no food, no stores and no money for that matter, laughing at his own joke.

That is when I say, "It's not funny," with my serious face. "Our families and neighbors are in that shelter." I put him on the spot, "Are you going to help me or not?"

Again being funny, Abud Alsalam says, "Well, if you put it that way, then I will."

Arising from bed in his underwear, he dresses in full military uniform, which is normal dress code in the camp. Once clothed, I ask him, "Where can we get food?"

I am counting on the connections I know his older brother has with the PLO.

"Well, I know a high-ranking PLO guy who we can explain the situation to. I know he can help."

We walk the streets of the camp under the roar of the Israeli jets flying overhead. Our destination, the office of Fatah, is one of the biggest divisions of the PLO. We see a large man, about six-four, 260 pounds with a dark beard, sitting behind the desk as we enter the office. His scarred face and mean appearance complete his scary profile.

I turn my head to Abud Alsalam, whispering, "Let's get out of here."

"I thought we are here to get food," he says.

"Man look at him, what food? He's going to eat us."

Abud Alsalam cannot help himself but to laugh, which draws the ominous attention of the man, who asks me, "Are you laughing at me?"

Not particularly scared and doubtful that he can help us judging by his looks, I say, "As a matter of fact, I am."

He stands, towering from behind the desk, demanding to know what has been said about him that made me laugh. I tell him exactly what I said and to my relief he laughs as well. I explain why we have come to his office, ending with, "Listen, I really, really need your help in this matter."

With no hesitation on his part, he says, "Sure, the people of the camp are my people. I am glad you came to see me because last night we received a shipment of bread and meat. Follow me."

We obey the large man and walk behind him to a big locked

metal door. From his right pants pocket he pulls a small key and unlocks the door. He shows us with a flashlight the whole legs of beef stacked high. Each leg is stamped with a blue ink symbol.

When I ask where they have come from, he replies, “Some East European country donated this meat to the PLO before Beirut was surrounded. Take as much as you can carry, it is spoiling anyway.”

I can affirm his last comment—the smell from the beef in the un-refrigerated room is rancid. Knowing I cannot even carry one leg, I ask, “What, do you think I am, Hercules?”

“Okay, I will send a couple soldiers with you in a truck.”

A green Nissan pickup is loaded down with four big legs of beef, filling the bed to capacity. He surprises me again with his kindness when he stops me, “Wait,” he says, leaving to return with about twenty five bags of pita bread.

He orders his driver to drop us and the food quickly at the shelter. As we unload the food, Abud Alsalam and I feel so good about our successfully accomplished mission of providing the shelter people with a week or more supply of food.

From that moment on I can tell I have earned the trust of the angel Rola. She walks to me and thanks us for going out of our way to help them.

Not long after that, around five p.m., the Israelis drop from an F-16 a thousand pound drum bomb on the camp near the shelter. The explosion shakes us like an earthquake, the whole earth collapses. Abud Alsalam and I run out of the shelter, seeing nothing but white smoke but hearing a woman screaming at the top of her lungs in a house close to where we are. We try to navigate, with our ears, through the smoke towards the screaming and as we go we step on limbless and decapitated bodies. Finally arriving at the house of the woman, we find her lying on her right side with her left leg completely chopped off, bleeding like an open water tap. While I kneel down to try to carry her to safety, something catches my eye—two little girls, or what is left of them—on the floor of the house where the smoke is clearing. Half of each wall is all that is left standing of the house. I manage to carry the woman in my arms out of the house, noticing then that her second leg is attached only by a vein or nerve, hanging. I stop and snatch the limb away, throwing it to the side of the street. Gaza hospital is a long way and I automatically start walking there still carrying the mother in my arms. Something inside me insists on trying to save her life, I risk my own for her sake.

Almost halfway to the hospital I notice she has stopped breathing. I put her down, trying to revive her and shaking her head, but there is no sign of life. I turn around, seeing a trail of blood far down the road. I announce her dead; I believe when it comes to pronouncing time of death, I have more experience than most doctors.

I sit on the ground next to her body, having a moment to myself, thinking why and what is happening to us. I turn my anger toward God, thinking all I hear around me is prayers to God, prayers asking him to keep they and their families safe, yet God is doing nothing to help. At the end of this moment I decide to forget about God completely and do whatever I can to help my people instead.

I shake myself from the experience, standing to return the way I had come. Heading back to camp I see the bodies lining

both sides of the street. I eventually manage to arrive back at the shelter. I lift the heavy metal handle of the basement door only to hear another woman crying and screaming at the top of her lungs. I cannot see the woman, only a crowd of sympathetic people standing around her as I slowly descend the steps. I make my way through the crowd, trying to find out what happened. The woman is my mother. She is hysterically slapping herself in the face, all I can do is kneel and try to calm her with an embrace. I ask the people what is going on, my mother cannot speak as she is exhausted from grief and crying. They seem reluctant to answer but eventually I learn that one of my older brothers had been killed a few hours earlier. A sniper had shot him just outside the camp.

I feel sorry for my poor mom who now feels the same pain of all the people who lost their own in this war. There is not one family in the camp that has not lost one, two, or three members; some families have been entirely wiped out. I have never seen my strong mother in so much emotional pain. I hold her still in my arms, not knowing what to say or do to bring her any solace; nothing but the return of her son could comfort her at this point. This does not keep me from eventually reminding her of her remaining seven sons, begging her to be stronger for our sakes.

At this a shaft of reason breaks through, she looks at me in a way I will never forget as long as I live, saying, "You are right. I am still one of the luckiest women in the camp."

She remembers the cumulative loss of all the families and finally begins to calm down. As I look over my right shoulder, Rola stands crying. I lay my mom down on her mattress, asking Rola to watch over her. She sits down next to my sedated mother, stroking her head as I storm outside the shelter. I have to get some fresh air—unfortunately no such air is to be found. The thick smoke always present outside leaves black spots under every nose. The only change I find outside is no change at all. There is death and destruction on all sides; the only freshness is the smell of blood and decay.

In one of the many narrow streets behind the basement, I sink down near what is left of a house and cry; he was my brother. My moment of grief lasts for almost an hour. While I cry, my friend Abud Alsalam comes up behind me, likely hearing my moaning and sobs from a distance. Not knowing what to say he stands for a few minutes, breaking the silence with, "I am sorry. I just heard that you lost your brother."

He tries to comfort me, reminding me of the same situation I was in with my mother.

"I have known you from when you could barely walk. This is the first time I have ever seen you cry."

As I look at his face I see that silent tears are already running down his cheeks. This is when I suggest that we stop crying. The tears of a man in public are one of the biggest shames, no matter how many of your family is killed. This is how we have all grown up. Abud Alsalam continues, "Listen, just try and remember, almost everybody we grew up with is either dead, dying, or waiting to be killed. We cannot cry for every single one of them can we? Where would we get enough tears? I promise you that all of us will die—look around you, do you see anything but death?"

This is when we shook hands in agreement that if either of us dies, we will not shed one tear. I feel stronger after this moment,

finding my feet again. We have never feared death anyway, as I am convinced I would not make it to the end.

In the middle of this conversation I see the most beautiful thing walking towards us, the angel of us all, Rola, who I see has sadness on her face. She speaks, “Your mom is okay now. She is asleep.”

She stands there and I feel from the message in her eyes she wants to speak with me alone. I ask my friend to excuse us for a moment. As I grab her left hand and walk away I tell Abud Alsalam, “We will be right back.”

We walk this way, her hand in mine, not paying attention to the danger of falling rockets and snipers around us. We walk all the way to the North end of camp, stopping and looking at each other once, only to turn around and continue our silent walk. As I think of what I have seen in her eyes before, I realize I misread her meaning; she had not wanted to talk to me, only to be with me. This I think is even better.

On the way back she stops suddenly and turns to face me, I think she has something to say. I wait for her to speak, but no word comes, she just reaches for my hand and walks before me leading the way to the shelter.

Outside the shelter is my friend still waiting for my return; Rola flinches, embarrassed it seems, for Abud Alsalam to see us still holding hands. Before we enter the basement she tells me, “You need to eat something, you are getting skinny.”

I wonder why she said this, am I actually skinny or does she not know what to say? My friend and I wait until she goes down into the shelter. I look at him and ask, “Am I really skinny?”

He says, “You’re just fine,” both of us smiling.

Curiously, Abud Alsalam asks what Rola and I had talked about. Even after having just lost my brother, I find myself laughing, answering, "Believe it or not, we did not say a word!"

I can tell from his expression that he has a hard time believing me, saying, "You were gone for more than half an hour, and not a word? Plus, you were with the most beautiful girl in the whole camp and you couldn't find anything to say to her?"

I assure him this is the truth, and because he has known me all my life he has no choice but to believe me.

Again he says, "I hope you know how lucky you are even to have a walk with her."

"I know," I say.

Abud Alsalam suggests, "Let's go to Gaza hospital and see what kind of action is going on."

Already I can tell he is bored.

"Alright," I answer, asking him to wait a few minutes while I check on my mother. I run down the steps to my mother and make my way to her corner, everything is calm and quiet, she lies in a deep sleep.

Rola walks to me as I look on, assuring me that my mother is in safe hands, and she asks, "You are staying, right?"

I tell her, "I have to go take care of some business."

"You can go if you promise me you will be safe."

Smiling, I remind her, "We are in Shatila camp, nobody is safe, but I promise not to put myself in harm's way, if that will help any."

We smile at each other again as I walk away.

Greeting Abud Alsalam who is still waiting, I give him the go-ahead with, "I am ready. Let's get going."

On the way to Gaza Hospital in the twilight, we see the wounded on the street and I suggest that we carry one of the unfortunates with us since we were going anyway. Angrily he assures me, "I am not carrying anyone to the hospital, if we have to carry one we have to carry all of them."

I feel his frustration and let the idea go. We keep on, finally reaching our destination. Many people and soldiers are gathered outside the hospital and we push our way through until we are inside the doors. Wounded soldiers line the floor. One soldier in particular, a young man in his mid-twenties with a severe head injury, has a two inch deep chunk missing from his forehead, leaving his brain exposed.

He screams, "Somebody help me, I am in a lot of pain!"

This kind of scene is normal to us. We see these kinds of injuries almost daily. We cannot help, but we can feel his pain. We ignore him and pass by to the second floor, where the action is; the second floor is the surgery level. Watching the doctors operate was shocking to us, it is not what we expected, we were expecting to see wounds being sewn, people being medicated. Instead, we see three soldiers holding a patient down on the metal operating table, his left arm and right leg being manually hack-sawed off, obviously without any pain-killer medication, as he is screaming loudly, "OOOOOOOOO!"

My friend and I can't help but gape at the pile of limbs next to the table, haphazardly tossed away. When they finish with this man, another is brought in and laid on the same table in the same pool of blood left from all the previous patients. This man receives the same treatment as the last. It did not take Abud Alsalam and I long to figure out that if the wound is in the arm or leg, the hacksaw is the only treatment available. We think that to be shot in the stomach or head is a greater mercy than to be wounded only in a limb, perhaps then the medical options are more kind.

Abud Alsalam turns his head to whisper in my ear, "If I am ever shot, don't bring me to this hospital. Just let me bleed to death."

"Maybe you will get lucky and get shot in the head, not in the limbs." I laughed sarcastically. Our laugh drew the doctor's attention, "Are you guys here to volunteer or just to laugh?"

This made us laugh even harder. The doctor became angry and kicked us out of the room, saying, "If you are not here to help you have to leave."

The funny thing is that this butcher-house of a hospital is run by Yasser Arafat's younger brother; he is the big butcher in charge. With such a powerful man in charge, there is no arguing policy; we think it is better if we leave, taking the stairs down to the lobby. We cannot help but notice the same man with the head injury lying unaided, still screaming. We notice his wound has stopped bleeding; he is near bleeding to death. The sad thing is that no one is paying attention to him, as if the poor guy does not exist. Abud Alsalam kneels down to whisper in the injured man's ear, he stands and I ask what he told the man.

He told me what he whispered, "May God have mercy on you because you are not getting any at this hospital."

I replied, "Maybe you should be the merciful one." He understands exactly what I mean.

He nods his head in agreement.

I take the man's arms and Abud Alsalam picks him up by his feet. We carry him out about fifty yards away from the hospital door. My friend pulls his nine millimeter handgun out from the back of his pants, loads a bullet in the chamber and asks me if I want the honor of putting the man out of his misery.

I reply with, "The honor is all yours."

The gun is aimed at his head, Abud Alsalam looks back and checks with me, he seems to have second thoughts as he asks if this is the right thing to do.

I assure him that he will die now or hours from now, we have to give this man some peace.

This is when my friend pulls the trigger and makes an end of the man's misery. After the mercy bullet we figure we have found more action than we bargained for. We decide to call it a day and begin heading back to camp. On the way home, after a couple hours of quietness, we hear the whistling of huge rockets starting to land in both Sabra and Shatila camps. We assume from the sound difference that the rockets must be different from what we are used to hearing, the launch and impact from far off signal the presence of aircraft carriers off the coast.

With this development, we add the new sound to our extensive knowledge of weapon identification. We have to take shelter as we are between the hospital and Shatila and a half-intact basement becomes our cover as we wait for the rocket storm to pass. While waiting we see the PLO vehicles loaded with soldiers speeding past going all directions. We assume they likewise are seeking shelter.

After an hour of waiting, the hammering of the camp is getting worse with no sign of letting up. Not able to wait any longer, we decide to make a run for it, zigzagging as we sprint and hitting the ground when a rocket lands nearby. Finally making it safely to the shelter, we open the heavy door and descend to the familiar chorus of women screaming and crying loudly.

We go through the process of finding out what is going on, quickly discovering that the last two of Rola's brothers have been killed. They lost their lives defending the capital city Beirut. This news shocks me. Rola lost her father not long ago in South Lebanon at the beginning of the invasion. Rola and her mother are the only two left of their once large family.

Rola's mother is a repeated scene of my mother not long ago, she kicks and screams uncontrollably. My eyes automatically search the large dim room for Rola. I spot her in a corner, crouched down hugging her knees and crying. I see her swollen eyes, wondering how long she has been crying this way. I feel the weight of her pain and suffering from the look on her face. My eyes follow her, not knowing if I should approach her or leave her alone to grieve. For a moment the helpless feeling returns. I could not bear to leave her without at least the comfort of my presence, as she had done for me not long ago. Finally I walk towards the corner, quietly seating myself next to her, not even attempting to speak. I want her to know I am there for her. Twenty-five minutes pass before she notices my presence. She crawls the few feet between us on her hands and knees, laying her head on my thigh.

Not thinking, I begin stroking her hair in an attempt to comfort her. After a few minutes I see that she is sleeping deeply; I do not move my numbing leg from under her for three hours.

Waking, she looks up to see if I am still with her, struggling to

give me a sad smile. I can tell she feels safer when I am with her. I am only too happy to have her head in my lap, feeling lucky once again despite the gravity of the situation. Rola's mother carries to her daughter a small meat sandwich, she pushes the offered food away, disgusted with the idea of it.

I take the sandwich from her mother's hand instead, hoping that I would succeed where her mother has failed. Rola has not eaten in two days. After some urging, Rola accepts the food but I see that the one choking bite she takes is a struggle. I feel rewarded by my accomplishment of getting her to take the one bite and the grateful smile of her broken-hearted mother at my limited success. I sense that Rola's mother needs to talk to her daughter in private; I stand and tell them I will be with my mother on the far side of the room if they need me.

I leave them both talking, crossing over to see how my mother is. I find her sitting on the mattress, crying, scared by the loud rocket explosions. Next to her, I wrap my arms around her shoulders, saying "Don't be scared, I am here. It isn't that bad outside," trying to abate her fears with a white lie.

She asks again, "Are there a lot of dead people on the streets?"

I continue with my lie, "Abud Alsalam and I just got back from Gaza hospital, there are barely any dead people on the streets."

She sees the lie in my eyes and bangs her hand on the back of my head, saying, "You are not a good liar."

I smile at her as I try to cover the falsehood with, "Truly, it is not that bad outside."

She catches my attention with news from a small battery-operated transmitter radio that reports the PLO have opened vacant schools as safe havens for the overflowing refugees. The schools are in central Beirut, I like the idea of moving my mother to a safer location away from the constant fire on Shatila. I ask the surrounding people if they would like to accompany us to the safer location, but the majority of families are unwilling to risk the journey with their small children. Two families of older couples agree to come. They have nothing to lose. I instruct them to pack their belongings for the trip in the morning. Among the circulating talk of leaving, the alarmed Rola comes to ask me if I am leaving the camp for a safer place. I take the opportunity to assure her that I will return as soon as I drop my mother and other families at the school.

I assure her again with a stronger promise, "I am going to be here for you to the end."

At the same time I feel compelled to ask why she cannot come with us, she replies, "Just me and my mom are left from our whole family. What reason do I have to leave? Plus, who will take care of and cook for the people left behind?"

I feel the strength of her will and let the subject go at her adamant claims that she will never leave the camp. It is late as Rola and I say good night and return to our respective sides of the basement, our eyes are locked even over the sea of heads between us. I lay beside my mother for the rest of the night, finding it hard to sleep with the thundering outside. I wonder what the Israeli army can be targeting at this late hour. Then somehow, I fall asleep.

In the early morning my mother wakes me with her rustling as she packs all our earthly belongings into a large green bed

sheet. Pots, pans and pillows, among other things, make the simple knotted knapsack rotund. I give my mother last minute instructions in rounding up the others while I head out to find Abud Alsalam, who will be our way out via his pickup truck.

In the morning stillness I emerge from the basement and run the familiar narrow streets to my friend's house. I find him already stirring in the house, his door open as is custom for an easy emergency escape. Abud Alsalam's family already resides in the school I hope to move my mother to. I yelled his name as I walked in the doorway. From his position on the floor near the couch, he tells me he is not deaf.

I tell him, "I need your truck. We need a ride to take my mom and some others to the refugee school."

He laughs; I ask what is funny only to have him laugh at me again. "There is no gas; this is why the truck has not moved for a while."

There are no gas stations in the camp. Fortunately, I have been smart even from childhood in such matters. The solution is simple. We need a hose and a container to siphon all the fuel necessary from the many damaged vehicles around the camp. Abud Alsalam wonders why he has not thought of this earlier. We proceed immediately with this idea, filling a five-gallon container quickly. After depositing the gas into his truck, we are ready for our mission.

We drive to the shelter, sit my mother in front and load the people and belongings in the back bed while I sit with the others atop the swaying mattresses. We travel this way peacefully, the only complications we encounter are the many rocket holes in the road that Abud Alsalam is forced to slowly navigate around. I call this 'driving slowly to get there fast,' any damage to the truck means being stranded and helpless.

Finally, we arrive at the large building. When we enter there are people everywhere. Children run around the innumerable groups of people who are cooking a menagerie of dishes. Smoke fills the room. We force our way among the throng and their mattresses, some of the residents are kind enough to make room for the new arrivals. A corner is carved out for my mother and the others who begin immediately situating themselves on their three mattresses which were carried by Abud Alsalam and I.

Soon we learn from the veterans around us that the PLO has provided some rations for the people here—rice, flour, and occasionally some meat. I am relieved to know that my mother will not be wanting for food.

Abud Alsalam excuses himself to visit his family who lives on the second level of the same building. It is not often that he gets the opportunity as the trip is perilous. I stay to speak with my mother before leaving. Of course she cries and begs for me to stay, feeling safer in this place and not willing for me to return to the danger of the camp. I remind her of the helplessness of the people still left in the shelter and that I am an able eighteen-year old who provides the only food they have. I tell her too many lives depend on my return. She understands.

I leave with her blessing while promising to visit every chance I get. In the back of my mind Rola is the strongest thing tying me to the camp, but I do not tell my mother that.

I wait outside next to the truck. Abud Alsalam tells me as he

comes later that he informed his family of my mother's presence and they have promised to look out for her.

Once inside the cab, I turn to ask him, "Why don't you stay with your family in this safer place. You have nothing at the camp?"

He looks directly at me, saying, "Well, I have you. If you stay I will stay with you here. If you go to the camp I go there with you. We are together to the end, aren't we?"

I reply affirmatively, "Yes we are."

He starts the engine and we discuss Rola as we ride back together. I did not want to talk, but with his cajoling it all comes out. I cannot hide the real reason for my return to the camp from him—we are open books to each other. He always understands me.

Half way back the rockets begin falling again. Striking nearby buildings, the flying debris hits the truck like a hail storm. The remainder of the trip is rough going but luckily we arrive back at the camp unscathed.

An old man outside the shelter delivers to us disturbing news; the family furniture store owned by Abud Alsalam's family is on fire, struck by a rocket while we were away. We drive straight south to the store, finding nothing left. The store is burned to the ground. Abud Alsalam and I sit on the sidewalk to watch the remaining flames die down in silence for an hour. There is no fire department in Shatila.

Finally I say, "The show is over, are you going to leave or are you going to sleep here next to the furniture store?"

"That is not funny," he replies, explaining the work that his father put into the business. He says his father will have a heart attack if he knows what has happened.

Being funny again I retort, “Look on the bright side. Nobody in this camp dies of heart attacks, only of rockets and snipers.”

He gives me a dirty look in disapproval of my comment: I am more serious with my next. “Really, your family is safe and that is what matters. The furniture place, it can be rebuilt, but for now let’s not die on the street like dogs. If we die, let’s die doing something useful.”

Agreeing, we rise and make our way back to the shelter in the truck. Once there, Rola comes running to me, obviously having waited nervously during my absence. I see happiness in her eyes and note her disregard of her mother’s disapproving look as she throws her arms around me. My happiness reaches new levels as I see that her affection is mutual. Along with her greeting she could not help but tell me that the people had not had much to eat that day.

Looking purposefully at Abud Alsalam who leans nonchalantly against the wall, cigarette in hand, he understands the look and seems frustrated that once again a new mission has arisen. I verbalize to him the people’s need.

He says, “I didn’t sleep last night, my brain isn’t functioning well. Why don’t you think of where to find food.”

I suggest we go from house to house. Those who left hurriedly from their homes are bound to have left something. So we go, finding jars of pickles, cans of tuna, corned beef, half-rotten loaves of bread, anything edible. In a small grocery store we locate about twenty abandoned cans of sardines. What we found was less than enough to feed the three hundred plus people in the shelter, but it is better than nothing. After six or seven hours of searching, we

return with our findings just in time for dinner so the people can eat something before bed.

Abud Alsalam and I have not eaten anything all day. The exhausted Abud Alsalam finds a cement corner to crash in, asleep instantly, using his left arm as a pillow. In the meantime Rola starts dinner with some other women. I see the people eating as a direct result of my labor and feel important to have provided it for them. Rola comes to serve me. I lie and tell her I have eaten already, afraid to take food that might be her dinner.

Under the watchful eyes of her mother, she takes my hand and pulls me away to the staircase where we sit and talk all night about everything. The candle light dims as people begin to sleep. Rola confesses her feelings for me. She tells me she has liked me from the first second she saw me. I confess as well, telling her that I felt the same when I first saw her.

We have stayed up all night talking and the time passes too quickly. It is the best time I have had since I was born. We pay no attention to anyone in the shelter, and give no mind to the explosions outside, we both hope this night will last forever. Unfortunately, nothing lasts forever.

The sun begins to rise and it is not long before we hear people in the streets screaming and running. I go out to investigate. Heavily armed PLO soldiers run everywhere carrying AK-47s and shouldering Russian made anti-tank B-7s. I pull one of the many soldiers aside to ask what is going on and am informed that the Israeli army traveling from the South has reached and surrounded Beirut this morning. The PLOs are loading in trucks, preparing for the front lines where they will face the Israeli army. I notice the majority of these men hugged farewells to each other, saying things like, "See you in heaven."

All have no illusions about their certain fate.

These scenes give me goose bumps. I know even at my age that these soldiers and their small firearms are no match for the heavily equipped Israeli forces. This does not sway any of them from their purpose. They choose death in choosing to defend their only home and people.

Soon after the departure of the PLO's we feel a difference in the atmosphere. Instead of a rocket per minute there are three or four rockets every minute. The Israeli army is closer. Their T-72 tank missiles directly hit the camp and nothing stops the increasing aircraft attacks that fly in over both neighboring camps. This keeps on for three days, non-stop, making it hard on anyone searching for food. I see clearly that there is no food at all left in the shelter. Even water supplies are gone. Three elderly people have died of hunger. Children cry constantly from their hunger pangs. The deprivation is so dire that safety precautions are abandoned, I see people heading out of camp on food searches in the heat of attacks. By the end of the day most of these do not return. I understand their reasoning in that it is better to die trying to live than to starve in a shelter.

Not long after this Rola comes to me with a radio update about another refugee camp about three quarters of a mile away from Shatila, Burj-el Barajneh camp, translated from Arabic as 'The tower of all towers.' The people there are reported to be eating everything moving on four feet, dogs, cats, rats, whatever they can find.

Some of the religious people airing on the radio say that this is okay in the Islamic religion to consume these animals under the circumstances. The news spreads among all the people of the camps, every animal becomes a target. My first hunt is a black cat, I am lucky to spot the feline among broken glass shards on a window sill. I try with all my might to catch the cat, both our lives equally in peril from the falling bombs. I corner the bristling, spitting animal and have no choice but to shoot it. One bullet from my nine millimeter in its stomach leads to its slow death fifteen minutes later. Victorious, I carry the still bleeding carcass by its back legs and run back to the shelter. I lay the animal on a coffee table next to Rola's mother and the women in the room gather around the prospective feast. I see in their eyes an amount of disgust which I defend with, "I promise you it tastes just like a rabbit."

Finally one of the stronger willed women declares, "Well, either we eat the cat or die of hunger, let's cook it and feed the children before they die."

Even so I know the meal will not stretch far for so many people. Rola comes to my side, not knowing what to say or think, I share my thoughts about the matter, the meal will only get to five percent of the people. I decide to go hunting again despite Rola's pleas that I stay, explaining that staying will be no benefit for anyone. I leave finally with her blessing, although we both know that everyone who leaves the safety of the shelter has a slim chance of returning.

Searching again through the camps for anything available or moving, it seems that the other hunters have already made quick work of all resident cats. After the long search I become dizzy and faint, not having eaten in four days, drinking only water and always giving my rations to those who have more need. I reach my breaking point, falling with the hunger knives stabbing in my stomach, even so my resolve not to return empty handed lifts me to my feet again.

I find myself in a field wooded with pine trees, Asass Field, at the end of the camp on Dalal El Mograbi Street in the area called Beer Hassan. I near the gate that fences in the field, hearing a growling noise as I approach. Inside the gate I draw my handgun and, still faint with hunger, I see the source of the noise. A brown spotted kind of German Shepherd is eating the entrails of a dead woman, intent on the meal with his whole head buried inside her torso, hidden from view. The dog did not seem to be starving, 120 or 130 pounds or more. Hearing my movement, he jolts his head up, growling through a bloody mouth.

I see only a feast, his threatening manner is no matter. I draw my still-loaded handgun, shooting once in his neck and once in the joint of his shoulder. I see the spray of blood at my success. The dog, still baring his teeth, takes menacing steps towards me. I shoot him twice more, missing once. The second bullet lodges in his abdomen, finally he turns and takes off running as if unaffected by his mortal wounds. I follow in chase, expending the last of my strength as the animal is my only chance of survival. Five-hundred yards later the distance between us lessens, the dog slows and drops to the ground, still crawling, his right paw clawing the earth as he nears death. Exhausted, I sit next to the dog, aim my gun again at his head, but stop at the sad eyes that meet mine. I lay my

gun next to me, deciding as I lean my back against a pine tree that he deserves to breathe his last without my mercy.

While waiting on the dog, I see a man moving from among the trees directly in front of me. He is carrying and AK-47, I see more clearly as he nears that he is a tall man, about six-foot-three and about 230 pounds. Blood covers his mouth, his neck, and his military uniform. I cannot tell if he is wounded or if he has been drinking blood. He aims his AK-47 at me, claiming the dog I shot is his. Of course I do not believe him, but at the moment I have no choice as his gun is bigger than mine. Adding to this his scary look, I feel this man will not hesitate for a second to shoot me, there is no law in Beirut and the man would never answer to anyone if he decides to kill me.

Not willing to take any chances, quickly I suggest, “Look, we can split the dog.”

Even with this compromise, I have already decided that I will not let him take the whole dog even if it costs me my life. Having one eye on the dog even as we talk, I see that the animal has breathed his last. The large man did not even consider my suggestion, asking, “Why would I do that?”

I tried to explain the hungry people in the shelter, saying that to share was the fairest solution. He instantly refuses. “You have a few seconds to decide, I am going to take the dog regardless.”

He does not wait for my answer before he kneels down to carry the dog on his shoulder. His eyes are watching me while he kneels, his gun lowers in the effort. In this moment I use all the energy left in me to pick up my gun and lunge at him, ending with the tip of my barrel at his temple, he is too slow to react. I see from his expression that he is shocked at my willingness to die for the dog.

Even in this vulnerable position he resists, dropping the dog and shooting three bullets into the trees and ground as he swings his gun towards me. With my left hand I grab the man's hand on the AK-47s handle and lower it while squeezing my gun to his head in earnest. Realizing his mistake, he screams, "Please don't shoot me!"

I instruct him, "Move away from the dog."

Backing three steps away, he says, "Sure, sure."

I remind him that it would have been better if he had agreed to take half the dog.

First he apologizes, then asks, "Can we still split the dog?"

At this moment I realize the stupidity of the man, answering in the negative, "No, you had your chance," as he continues to plead for half.

Obviously not trusting the man, I watch and keep my gun trained on him while picking up his by the leather strap, swinging it over my head to my back. I am not willing to take the chance of the man pursuing me or pulling out another weapon so still facing him I shoot his right knee cap twice. I hear the bone break and he crumples to the ground, cursing profusely and assuring me he will find me and do awful things to my family

I feel his cursing is a deliberate provocation; he is counting on me to shoot him so as to be put out of his misery. His chances of getting help in this remote location are close to none. I am unwilling to give him such satisfaction, at this moment my logic wins out over my natural inclination to give him mercy. I opt to leave him with at least a slim chance of survival. Before leaving I ask if he is hungry, he sarcastically barks back, "Damn right I'm hungry, why do you think I am willing to die over a dog?"

I pull from my back pocket a razor sharp six-click knife, a popular fighting knife that makes six clicking noises when opened in a half-circle. Everyone in the camps, including the soldiers and the elderly carry this popular back-up weapon.

I shove my nine millimeter in the front of my pants, kneel next to the dog, knife in hand and slice the dog's right thigh open, removing a large chunk of flesh, about a pound and a half. Considerate enough to not dirty the meat, I place the slab on the belly of the dog, slicing and dicing it into half inch cubes. With my right hand I grab a handful of the chunks and carry them to the man's lap, my left hand is filled with my own portion. A five foot gap between us, I sit with my left hand full of my own portion, waiting for the motivation of seeing him eat first to stomach the raw meat. I need the energy, my vision is blurring and I am seriously doubting I can carry the dog any distance. The man stares across the space, testing me by asking, "You are tough enough to shoot a big guy like me but not to eat dog meat?"

To prove myself, I take two chunks from my hand, shoving them in my mouth. As I begin to chew, the raw meat is tough and slimy, tasting sour with a slightly sweet aftertaste. The man follows suit, we watch each other as we proceed to eat the flesh, taking second helpings until everything is gone.

Resting from the meal, I feel my strength returning. I watch the still-bleeding right knee of the man, not wanting to dwell on this, only on my mission of getting the meat to the people of the shelter. I stand bidding the man farewell and good luck with his situation. I carry the dog on my left shoulder. I begin to leave when he calls out, "You are just going to leave me here?"

I retort, “What, you think I am your friend now?” as I continue to walk away carrying my prize. Feeling stronger as I go, I stop at a vacant house to butcher the rest of the dog, not wanting the people in the shelter to be see the actual animal.

I lay the dog on the living room floor, searching in the kitchen for a suitable knife. Finding a large blade with a black handle, I face some difficulties in cutting its head off, ending up skinning the entire neck before successfully separating its head from the rest of the body.

I continue skinning, deeply opening the belly, seeing the contents of the stomach. Fingers and other faintly recognizable human parts greet my eyes, all I can do is gut the stomach and intestines. I am glad already that I had not brought the dog straight to the people.

I separate the meat from the bones and several hours later the dog is a clean-boned skeleton. I place the meat beside me on the rag rug, locating a black bed blanket when I finish. I carefully arrange the large chunks weighing approximately a pound each in the middle of the blanket, tying a bow knot to secure the food. Now carrying the bundled blanket, I toss the AK-47 on what was left of the dog, having no further need of it.

Walking back towards my goal, I see in the street people screaming in mortal pain from wounds. I meet an eight or nine year old girl clothed in black and white striped pants and a black T-shirt, covered in blood, her mother dead two feet away. Moving closer, I see more clearly that the pools of blood around her head are from two holes in her neck and chest. I drop the blanket and kneel next to her, looking at her mouth open and close mutely. I

feel unbidden tears rolling down my cheeks, the first ever for an unknown wounded person.

Her face is beautiful, long black hair soaked in her own blood. I lift her head to my lap and gauge with my finger how deep her neck wound is and feel one of her vertebrae splinter as I do, knowing she will be paralyzed even if she does survive.

While I consider this, a shadow falls next to me. An old man is back dropped against the sun. He is bald with neatly trimmed gray hair around the sides. He looks down at me and asks, "What are you doing? Save yourself, she will die anyway."

He is right, rockets still fall even as we speak. I tell him, "I don't want her to die alone, I want to be here with her when she dies."

He says, "God is with her, she is not alone. Who will be with you if you die here? Young man, go find your shelter, don't be in the streets."

I stand, asking him what we should do for her pain. Pointing at my gun, he suggests, "Why don't you put her out of her misery?"

"I cannot do it," I reply, passing the handle of my gun to him. "If you have the heart for it, you do it."

He takes a second look at the girl, giving the indication that he is thinking about it. He says, "Okay, Okay I'll do it," as tears brim in his own eyes. Heartbroken, he takes the awful responsibility on himself. The old man puts the gun close to her head, his hand shaking terribly.

I grab his hand, asking, "Are you sure you can do this?"

"Yes, yes," he assures me.

Then I see the girl's eyes following the gun, I scream for him to stop. I kneel down again, lifting her body with my left hand under her back, her head falling sharply backward. I cover her eyes with my other hand, instructing the old man, "Now," and seeing his hand still shaking.

He looks down on me, fearfully asking, "What if I shoot your hand by mistake?"

I have him put the gun on the side of her head, clear of my hand, on her face.

He shoots one single shot, spraying both of us with blood as he does. I lay her body on top of her mother's. Turning, I see the old man shaking with the gun still in his hand, crying violently. I embrace him, he cries as he rocks back and forth, "May God forgive me, may God forgive me."

I assure the old man we have done the right thing under the circumstances, not knowing if I even believe my own words. These events now over, I ask the man what he was doing out of doors. He is hungry, his family left four days ago and he does not know where they are.

I automatically untie the blanket and pull a large chunk of the dog meat out, placing it in his hands. Staring blankly, he then asks what kind of meat it is. I reply, "The kind that will keep us alive."

"You are absolutely right, it is better even not knowing what kind of meat," He replies, answering his own question.

I tell the old man to return home, to get off the streets. Before leaving, he says, "May God bless you, I know your father—he is a good man."

I thank him and we walk away in opposite directions.

The shelter is only a few hundred yards away and I lift the

door and descend. Once down, I see the people huddled into one corner, terrified of the rocket attack. They break from the group upon seeing me, knowing my return means food. I lay the blanket on the ground, distributing the meat to the gathered circle around me to cook as they see fit. One woman screams and stops the process, insisting that all the meat be returned so that it may be cut up precisely, everyone getting an even share according to their family's size.

With this going on, I am drawn to the PLO radio station named WAFA, tuned in somewhere in the room. This station only plays revolutionary songs and from time to time a news update from the front lines of the conflict with the Israeli army. I leave the people to the meat and take a break from the ever-present news stories.

I step outside, looking forward to a cigarette break after the long day. I cannot help but notice as I smoke that the number of armed people out in the open has significantly decreased. Most able bodied men are on the front lines, leaving only a handful of PLO's left to defend the camp. The emptiness of the camp, the dead bodies on the street, these strike in me a realization of the seriousness of this war, it is unlike any I have experienced in my life.

Still smoking, I wonder how much longer this will last, how many more people will die before this war ends. The scarcity of food leads me to believe that starvation may finish us off before the Israeli army does. These thoughts still going through my head, Rola comes out to join me, breaking my reverie.

"Thank you for bringing us food," was the first thing she said.

As I expected, she asked the question I was not looking forward to answering, "What kind of meat is that?"

I put a smile on my face and with full confidence reply, “It is cow meat.”

At this she turns, takes my face between her hands so my eyes have to see hers and smiles back, but is unconvinced. Perhaps not wanting the truth, she is satisfied enough not to question me further.

“Then that is a very small cow,” is her only reply.

My silent smile again went unchallenged.

Still holding my face, she says the three words that make my whole body weak. My knees go wobbly, I almost fall back when she tells me she loves me. Out of nowhere and completely unexpected, the half-finished cigarette drops from my hand. I am speechless, having lost all expressive ability. I am no longer subject to gravity it seems, almost flying from excessive happiness. She is every man’s dream. I am so drawn to her beauty, now even more I am drawn to the beauty of her personality. Caring not only for her mother, but also for all the people in the shelter, her small frame contains the largest heart I have ever known a person to possess. Such beauty in such an ugly war leaves me breathless.

She lets my face go, waiting silently in anticipation for me to answer her. I am overwhelmed, for some reason I cannot say the words. Her bravery in exposing herself this way to me is slightly emasculating, her strength outstrips my own and I am still too shocked to react appropriately. As we stand in this indefinite pause, I know I am so in love with this girl. She is the reason, after all, that I am taking responsibility for the people in the shelter. She is the reason why I am alive, not fighting and dying in the doomed war with other boys my age. She is the reason why any happiness survives in my soul.

Still talking hours later, I find myself promising to marry her when this war is over. She promises herself to me as my bride and in the lull of the evening under the open sky we give each other hope, binding our promises with a holy oath. Agreeing on this, the time passes so quickly we can hardly believe it is almost four in the morning. The only thing concretely marking the time is the peeking head of Rola's mother who checks on us from time to time. She is not worried for her daughter with me, but for both of our safety outside.

I look into Rola's tired eyes, telling her the truth of the time, begging her to go rest. She refuses to leave me and after asking twelve or more times, I finally convince her to go but with great reluctance. I know for a fact she will be needed to help cook in the morning and as for myself I have not slept in the past four days. She agrees at last, promising me before she leaves that she will eat something before bed, procuring a promise from me earlier that I had also eaten that day. When she leaves I walk to the nearest house to lie down on some stranger's bed. One of the cardinal rules I would be ashamed to break is for a man to sleep with the women and children in a shelter. It would be the talk of the camp if such a thing were to happen.

Despite my exhaustion, my mind repeats over and over the exquisite three words given to me by Rola. They are the peace of my sleep and the smile on my lips. As soon as I drop off, a blinding explosion throws me off the bed to the floor. Even with my eyes closed I still sense the intense brightness of the explosion. The impact is one or two houses away.

I am so exhausted, I simply climb back in bed to finish my

peaceful dreams, thinking to myself that I will not move from this bed unless a rocket hits me straight. Yet in the back of my mind I know that Rola is outside the shelter trying to make sure that I am alright. This alone moves me outside to check if my premonitions are correct. Sure enough Rola and her mother are outside searching, her mother spots me first. Rola runs to me while crying hysterically, I soothe her with, "I am like a cat with seven lives. Plus, I am not going to die, I promised to marry you. I cannot die before then."

As I say these things I am shepherding both of them back to the shelter with open arms afraid of a second rocket hitting nearby. Once I manage to get them both on the steps Rola's mother comes back to plant a kiss on my forehead. She tells me, "I have already lost two sons. Don't let me lose my last remaining one."

This is the sweetest thing this woman could ever have said to me. I appreciate it even as I deny Rola's pleas that I stay with them in the shelter. Even for her I could not bear the shame of staying with the women and children.

I return again to the same bed, eyes only half open. My body slams into bed, waking at eleven later that morning to find myself in a pool of my own sweat.

The summer morning promises to become a red-hot day. I step out of the house, blinking at the fresh rubble of houses that had stood nearby only the night before. A few more steps outside I see Rola also looking for me with tears in her eyes. Coming to her I ask why the tears. She replies, "Because of you, I got worried about you, I thought that I lost you."

This makes me smile. "Not me, I am not going to die so stop

crying. Plus it looks like a beautiful day. I don't want to die and miss it."

She speaks peace again to me, repeating herself from last night, "I love you so much."

That said, I realize what a beautiful morning it is to wake up to. I again cannot answer her in kind, beginning to feel rakish but being unable to help myself. I try to change the subject, "Well, is there enough food for the people to eat today?"

She pauses, catching the significance of my change of subject. I did not mean to insult her intelligence, being fully aware of her faculties.

She allows me off the hook, answering, "No, there is no food beyond lunch."

I say, "Don't worry my love, I will find some food." I give her cheek a kiss before I go off, not leaving before I see her face turn scarlet in a matter of seconds. This stolen kiss violates the religious and moral beliefs of our culture. To allow me such freedom proves her love for me. If her father had seen the kiss we both would be shot. Walking away, I feel the heat of her eyes watching. A hundred-feet later, I quickly turn to affirm that she still watches and this inspires in me confidence of the strength of our feelings for each other. Under the beautiful sun I head to Abud Alsalam's house and once in the doorway I see him on the couch calmly cleaning an AK-47 with olive oil.

"I did not know you owned an AK-47."

"Well," replied he, "I might be needing it soon."

"Are you cleaning it with olive oil?"

"Yes, it is the best thing for this kind of weapon."

I laugh, "What, are you an expert now? They have special kind of cleaning oil."

"Well, it was the only thing I could find."

I exclaim, "Tell me that then! Anyway, where have you been hiding?"

He explains that he had to deliver some summer clothes to his family at the school. Asking about my mother, he says he checked on her before his own family. She is well and asking about my safety and Abud Alsalam placated her with news of me staying safe at the shelter.

Abud Alsalam tells me of my brothers who have been visiting her fairly frequently.

As usual, I tell him I need his help. Sarcastically he retorts, "Anything for you Sunshine."

"I am serious." I reply.

On the same key he answers back, "So am I."

"We have to find food for the people of the shelter."

"Do you know I spent half the night looking for cats, dogs, rats…there is no food!"

I reply, "Yes, there is food, plenty of it."

Laying his AK-47 aside and standing, he says, "Please tell me where."

"Do you remember the basement of Al-Jaliel school?"

Hardly letting me finish my sentence, he exclaims, "God-damn-it, how could I forget that!"

He knows my thoughts exactly, as always. Our feet quickly take us to the deserted school we know so well. We stop to gape at the bombed playground, craters are everywhere, pipes are exposed.

Adjusting to the sight we move on, the only thing that matters is the integrity of the basement. Ignoring everything but this, we find plenty of what we are looking for; big juicy rats. Abud Alsalam looks at me saying, "I think we just hit the jack pot."

"Alright, I will try and find something to load the rats in."

The janitor's room is right next to the basement door. I dig around and find big plastic industrial sized mop buckets labeled "Caution, slippery floor." Grabbing two of these I also pick up two sets of thick yellow rubber gloves. The gloves smell bad, but we need them for the job. Returning to the basement I hear the anger of my friend before I see him. He is cursing as he rounds up and kills the rats, one of them has bitten a chunk out of his right pointing finger. Bleeding badly, he holds his hand up to show me. Even though I can see straight to the bone I find the situation hilarious.

"That's not funny! It hurts like Hell! I might get gangrene!"

"What, first you are a weapons expert and now a medical expert?"

"Let's see what you will do if a rat bites your finger!"

During his last outburst I reach down to show him the rubber gloves. Angrily he snatches them from my hands, putting them on.

"How do you feel now?"

"I feel great now, I am ready to get my revenge on those rats."

"Good," I reply, "Get as much revenge as you can because we need to fill those containers."

I stand by for two or three minutes to watch as Abud Alsalam spends his anger on the rats, grabbing one at a time to throw them as hard as he can against the cement wall, breaking every bone in their bodies. Once smashed the rats are picked up by the tail, being deposited in the yellow containers. Having enough of the show, I decide to join the rat massacre. Imitating the success of my friend, I chase the oversized rats, which are easier to catch than normal due to their wide girth. At the end of the bloodshed we totaled about 147 rats, all that the buckets could take. We carry them outside the school and cross our arms in contemplation.

Abud Alsalam asks finally, “Are we really going to eat these rats?”

“How much choice do we have?”

Soon a small crowd congregated around us, realizing there is food. We are swift to explain the source, nervous that our catch will be confiscated if a fight breaks out in the camp. Everyone is near starving, everyone also has a gun. We carry the containers away with fast steps, heading straight for the shelter with no time to disguise the meat’s nature this time. Arriving there, I ask Abud Alsalam to stand guard outside with the buckets while I go explain to Rola. Spotting her listening to the radio, she runs to me as soon as she sees me. I tell her hesitantly, “I found food, but I don’t know if you will like it.”

“If it is edible, we will be just fine.”

“Come up with me, it is upstairs.”

“If you don’t want to bring it down here it must be really gross. What is it?” she asks while dragging her feet, being conflicted about actually discovering what I have brought.

Upon her insisting, I answer, “It’s rats.”

Her hand covers her mouth in disbelief, still following me to Abud Alsalam and the containers. She peers inside, politely saying, “Well, they are meaty.”

Probably she is hungry, perhaps this softened her otherwise outright disdain.

"Okay," said she, "I will find something to cover them."

I grab her arm and ask once again if this is really okay. She says, "Well, the people downstairs are about to die of hunger, at least now they will have something to eat." She leaves only to return a few minutes later with a plastic table cloth and the same pragmatic woman who insisted on dividing the dog meat evenly.

When this woman took a look at the rats, she said, "Well, we cannot bring this down there, there are children."

She brilliantly suggests that she and Rola adjourn with the rats to a vacant house to skin and clean them. I feel this is too large a job for the sensitive Rola, but the nature of the task is too womanly for me to offer help. They begin skinning and chopping to disguise the shape of the animal and once finished the meat is returned to the same containers and Abud Alsalam and I are called away from our cigarettes to help carry them down to the people. We stand for half an hour watching while Rola and the women fill two huge stew pots with the meat, adding rice as it cooks. They are cooking rat rice soup.

"Now," says Rola calmly, "we can tell the people it is chicken rice soup."

As she starts serving, everyone brings their bowl to be filled. When it came to Abud Alsalam and I, we accept the soup, and immediately my friend begins eating the meat. Out of courtesy or hunger, I am not sure, Rola, the woman and I watch everyone around us eat and, encouraged we begin eating as well. After a few bites I figure it is not all bad. It tastes exactly like chicken. We enjoy the good meal together.

Abud Alsalam and the strong willed woman have developed a rapport, they strike up a lengthy political conversation. Meanwhile I take the opportunity to pull Rola aside while we finish our soup. I am always looking out for stolen moments with her. I commend her heroic work in transforming the ugly situation into a sweet one. Her fortitude benefits everyone. She never stops working and caring for us all even as things get worse. I tell her, "You are the perfect model of a hero."

She turns this back on me, calling me the hero for accepting the responsibility of providing food for the people. I have no choice as I confess, "I am no hero, I only take the responsibility to be around you and to be with you."

As I confess I add that this makes me selfish more than anything, to take care of people as a means to an end. Trying to salvage her compliment, she says that this makes me an even bigger hero than she thought. No matter the motivations, if my love causes hundreds of people to be cared for, that in itself is noble. There is no winning with this girl, I end the conversation with a smile. During our speeches my heart pounds with a preoccupation, I desperately try to muster the courage to tell her the three words my heart is dying to say. With all the love I feel for her, I still fail to say it. Rola senses the importance of my silence, asking, "Is there something you want to tell me?"

Still having no words, I unwillingly lie, "No, nothing."

Although I cannot tell her everything, I do manage to say how beautiful she is, assuring her of my commitment to our future. Her mother's voice calls her away, saving me from myself.

CHAPTER TWO

Nothing Left to Eat but...

Fifty-three days have passed since the Israeli army's invasion of Lebanon, forty-seven days have passed since the surrounding of the dying capital city Beirut. No food or medical supplies have been permitted through the siege and the circumstances become more obscene with each passing day. It is more likely now to be struck by lightning than to find anything to eat. I am as committed now to saving the people in the shelter as I was that first day, even though the job is now impossible. No animal has escaped becoming a meal. There is nothing left.

Even among all this starvation, an elderly man in the shelter comes up with the ingenious idea of running the TV off a car battery with the antennae wired through the roof. Two channels from Syria and Egypt barely come in on the small black and white screen. For the first time we have a window outside the camp. The violent pictures from the front lines are disturbing, none the less it is good that our isolation is broken. Each day the man runs the immobile car's engine briefly to conserve its gas as the battery charges. For fifteen minutes each evening the people crowd around the set, eager to see what is going on in the war.

From the Egyptian channel one day I hear the Imam (an authority on Muslim law) from Al Azhar University, one of the largest Islamic universities in the Middle East. He makes a fatwa, a pronouncement of approval and blessing, that it is now permitted by the Islamic religion for the people of Beirut to eat the dead human bodies. The same Imam mentions that in Burj-el Barajneh, one of the biggest Palestinian refugee camps in Beirut, they have already begun to do so. Hearing this makes a lot of sense to me, I walk away from the whispering people and go outside for a cigarette to think more about this idea. I need to consider if I can do this or not, I soon realize that I am more willing to keep these people from perishing than to hold scruples about what I will or will not do. If I become a human butcher in the process of saving them, so be it.

Abud Alsalam interrupts my thoughts. He is visibly thinner than last time I saw him. I think this is funny as I pull on his loose pants and ask how much weight he has lost.

Not feeling as jovial as I, he looks seriously at me, saying, "It's not funny."

"You are right," I say, "It's not funny, how long has it been since you ate something?"

"To be honest, I don't remember. If it makes any difference, I haven't been to the bathroom for more than a week."

"That is too much information. I didn't need to know that."

I tell him that I need to discuss something with him.

"What is it?" He asks.

"First I want to ask you, are you a man or a little boy?" I propose, using a kind of reverse psychology.

With a stoic face he asks, "How can you ask me something like this, after all we have been through and all the things we have eaten? And now you ask me a question like that?"

"I had to make sure. What I am about to ask of you is more than I can personally bear."

"Is it that serious? Should I be worried of what you are about to say?"

"No…maybe…I don't know."

He tells me just to say it.

"Look around, what do you see?"

"Rubble"

"And what else?" I ask.

"Dead bodies."

At this I stop him with, "Ahh!"

He tires of my game, asking, "Would you stop beating around the bush. Just tell me straight what it is you want me to do this time. You have made me do the craziest things possible in this lifetime, just spit it out."

I point at the dead bodies, saying, "Do you see all these? We are going to turn them into food."

He looks silently at me as though I have lost my mind, then asks, "Are you serious?"

I stop again to let the idea sink into his head and before answering I say, "Give me another choice and I will listen."

Cussing, he yells, "God-damn-it you are serious!" answering his own question.

He walks away, hands waving still yelling.

"That's it. You have lost your mind completely. I don't want to be part of this."

I pull him back by the collar, reminding him of his manhood, saying that now he was acting like a boy.

"That's it. I've made up my mind, I would rather die of starvation than eat human flesh."

"That is your opinion, but what about the people downstairs? Are you telling me they would rather die too?"

He stops to face me again, I pull a pack from my pocket and offer him a cigarette, hoping this will calm him. With a sad smile, he informs me, "I just want you to know that I regret your friendship," even as he accepts the cigarette.

I test this last statement, "Would you take a bullet for me?"

"*You* will take a bullet for me!" He fires back.

"I will take two bullets for you," I said.

"Have you seen the bullets these days, eight inches long, all you need is one."

After this amusing conversation he becomes serious again, asking for some time to gather his thoughts.

"Alright," I say, "take all the time you need. I am going to be down in the basement talking to the only girl who can understand me."

Walking down the steps, I hear the people still talking about the shocking subject Abud Alsalam and I just finished with. Some of

them were saying they could eat anything. Others are adamant that they would rather starve than eat human blood.

Rola comes towards me, stopping directly before me.

"It's okay, you have done everything you can for us, I know for a fact there is nothing else you can do. Maybe we should leave it to God at this point."

She could only have meant that maybe it was time to give up and die. I tell her, "If God could do something he would have done it already. Listen to me. We are not giving up. Do you see the rubble outside? We can't eat those cement blocks. I have a better idea but need you to understand it."

I draw her attention to the subject that everyone is discussing. She is serious and unbelieving as she asks, "You aren't thinking of feeding us human flesh are you?"

"First let me ask you," I say quickly, "are you my girl?"

This breaks the seriousness of her face with a smile.

"Forever I am your girl."

"You had better be, because I can't live without you."

I have to stop playing around saying, "There is a lot of food, all over, all around us. I want you to think of it as a temporary situation."

Still unable to fathom the idea, she says, "You feed us cats, dogs, rats, and now humans? What comes after humans?"

"Don't worry about that, we will never run out of food ever again. Have you seen all the dead bodies outside?"

"Okay, I will feed it to these people," waving at the people around her, "as long as you don't bring the whole body down here, just the meat."

Relieved at her acquiescence I say, "Well, I had better get to work then."

As I turn to leave, she catches my right hand, "Are you sure we are going to do this?"

I understood her hesitation. The idea is horrible but necessary. She wishes me luck holding my hand as I try to walk away. I have to whisper, "Let go."

Anxious to know Abud Alsalam's verdict, I take the stairs up in a run. He is no where in sight, I walk out further and see him kneeling down in the middle of a small side street. A dead woman wearing a black head scarf and robe is the object of my friend's deep thought. I approach from behind. He is so intent I think he does not notice me. I stand only a foot away when he looks up from his position over the woman, telling me, "No women."

"What?" I ask.

"We are not going to eat women, or children for that matter."

I am elated that this is the only condition to his participation.

"Deal." I say.

Abud Alsalam rises from his knees and as we walk side by side down the narrow walk, he asks me to fill him in on what I planned to do. I begin….

"First of all, me and you have no idea what we are going to do, but I know where to start."

I relate to him what the Egyptian Imam had announced on the TV, telling him that the residents of Burj-el Barajneh had been eating humans for a while now. That is where we are going to start, we will go to Burj-el Barajneh to learn the process.

He exclaims "What do you think? There is a school to teach you how to chop up a human?"

"It's not school, it's a process." I insist.

"Okay let's go there. What is the plan to get there, you don't expect me to walk a mile and a half on my feet do you?"

"No, we're going to hitch hike. There are so many military trucks going there all the time."

We make our way to the main street, the same one that leads to the airport and to Burj-el Barajneh. We do not go far before a PLO vehicle stops to ask us where we are going. We tell them our destination and the man in the passenger side motions for us to hop in the back, they are headed the same way. About seven fully armed soldiers already ride in the bed and they move to the side as we climb up. Right away we see that the soldiers are in the middle of lunch, sardines and pita bread are being eaten with their fingers. The sacks of bread and cans lay on the floor of the truck between us. Abud Alsalam could not keep his mouth shut, asking, "Where did you guys get this food?"

That said, one of the guys opens a can of sardines for Abud Alsalam and another for me. Pieces of pita bread are passed to us as and the sandwich I make of it is not easy to eat on the bumpy ride, but the bread never tasted so good. This pita bread has always been our staple. In our culture any dish is accompanied with it and we have not seen it in a long time.

While we eat, we listen to the soldiers' stories of the front lines. One of them proudly tells us he had killed two Israeli soldiers in the last confrontation in White Sands, an area called El Rawsha. Each soldier feels as though his story must top the last. The next man relates that he took an Israeli soldier prisoner, but some soldiers from an armed group not belonging to the PLOs, the

Amal movement, took possession of his prize. Unwilling to fight for it, he let them take the captive. Everyone laughed at this story calling the soldier a coward. The brave and courageous boasting continues until we reach our destination. We are dropped in front of a movie theatre in the middle of Burj-el Barajneh camp.

We walk in the streets, unsure of where to start.

Eventually we stop a soldier passing by and explain our purpose for coming. He is kind enough to take us to the human butcher house, saying, "Follow me."

We notice this larger refugee camp is more heavily guarded than Sabra or Shatila. It is nearer to the airport which is the closest base for the PLO against the most likely starting point of an invasion. This is the front line. Military trucks under shelter, hidden from Israeli fighter jets, are loaded with Katuosha rocket launchers in the beds, holding twelve rocket-filled pipes.

We continue to follow our guide as two rockets simultaneously hit behind us over the ground we just passed. We are thrown four or five feet by the explosive force. White smoke and fine cement dust choke the air and I scream Abud Alsalam's name to make sure he is alright.

He yells back, "I'm alright, I'm alright!" Fortunately none of us were wounded.

When he comes close enough to see, I notice the dust has powdered him white. He has the appearance of a seventy-year-old man; white moustache, hair, and eyebrows. I break out laughing, telling him, "You look like an old man with this gray hair!" pointing to his chalked head.

"You should take a look at yourself!" he counters.

Our guide is shocked by our levity, he holds his fingers close together, saying, "We were this close to being killed and you guys stand here laughing?"

Abud Alsalam becomes defensive, telling the man, "We are still alive, aren't we? That is something to celebrate."

We keep walking and Abud Alsalam makes another comment, "You notice there are not as many dead bodies on the streets here like in Shatila camp."

I reply, "Maybe they ate them all."

This starts us laughing again, bringing our guide to the end of his patience, "You guys are crazy."

He indicates that he will go no further with us by stopping and pointing his finger to a place about three-hundred feet away. He says, "Do you see that white building?"

Seeing the way, we do not feel that badly that he has left us. Making our way to the building, we see children gathered around outside, they watch the end of the street where the rockets recently hit.

I ask one boy who is in charge here and he snaps, "In charge of what?"

"Alright," I say, "who is in charge of the building then, who is the main man?"

"That would be Abu Hadeed (the father of iron in Arabic)."

"Where do we find him?"

"He is downstairs."

Following his instructions, we find ourselves in a basement shelter about three times bigger than the one in Shatila housing. There are roughly twelve-hundred people in the large room. Most of these are eating, we have arrived at mealtime. We stop another boy, asking for Abu Hadeed. He says, "Follow me."

He takes us to a room at the end of the shelter screened by a black bed sheet that is pulled back as we enter. The only light in the place comes from a few small barred windows that have long since lost their glass. We see a man standing at a table stripping the meat from a human leg. Extremely dark, his skin could pass for a black man's. He is tall, heavy set with a bald spot on his crown that is hemmed in by curly dark hair. My friend and I look at each other. We have come to the right place.

We ask the man, "Are you Abu Hadeed?"

"That depends," he says importantly.

This makes me smile, a butcher with a sense of humor. He returns the smile and we introduce each other while he apologizes for not shaking our hands. His arms are bloody to the elbows.

Abu Hadeed never ceases his work, as he fills the large trays next to him on the floor with slabs of meat. The bones are cast on another pile in the corner. We ask, "Can we have your attention for a little while?"

"Well," he says "I am about done, this is the last leg I am working on."

We wait four or five minutes until he finishes, then watch him rinse his hands in a basin filled with red water, wiping the pink excess on the olive drab army shirt he wears.

"Let me give you guys a quick tour here," he says congenially.

This offer seems strange in that the place is just one big room, but we agree, not wanting to ruin his attempt at hospitality.

We wind between the people on the mattresses as he

announces, "You see these people eating? They are eating God's made human flesh."

He takes us to the far end of the room where about twelve mattresses lean against the wall.

"See those mattresses, all those people who slept on those since yesterday died. They are probably the ones we are eating now!"

The man is weirder than we thought; the more we know of him, the stranger he becomes. Abud Alsalam leans in to whisper, "What does he think, we've never seen a dead body before?"

I quiet him with, "Shut up and listen so we can get through with this."

I did not want to give Abud Alsalam a chance to offend the man as he did with our last guide. At the end of the short tour I stop the guy in the middle of the floor. "Look, you probably think we are tourists here."

He gives me a strange look wondering I am sure why I am interrupting his speech. I continue, "We are here to learn how to prepare human flesh for food. We left a lot of starving people in Shatila and we would appreciate it if you would get down to business."

"Well I am just trying to be nice," he explains.

"I appreciate what you are trying to do."

"Okay, have it your way. Follow me."

We return with him to the same room where we first met and he begins our instruction.

"We should start with a fresh body then."

He yells to a couple of helpers, asking them to bring him a fresh body. They return several minutes later carrying a soldier in fatigues. They lay him on the table, backing away several feet while lighting up their cigarettes to watch the familiar show. Abu Hadeed expertly strips the man naked with his sharp kitchen knife. The body has three holes in the chest from bullets or shrapnel I cannot tell but this is not a concern.

He proceeds, “This is the thing, when our heroes die they end up on this table.” He chases this with a sick joke and a loud laugh, “Well, if we don’t eat them, the worms will!”

He begins his lesson with, “First of all you have to look at the body as meat if you don’t think of it this way you will be sick to your stomach.”

He slits the torso open from under the rib cage to below the navel, reaching his hand into the cavity, pulling the contents out all together, dropping them between the legs of the body as he cuts them free. He shows us a small white organ from below the liver, “You see this, make sure not to cut this by mistake, the whole body will be ruined if its contents leak out. The rest is easy, just cut it up the way you want.”

He mentions, “I will give you guys some advice, don’t try to eat the meat raw, always cook it or you will get sick. I’m going to show you my favorite part to eat.”

He rolls the body over onto its stomach, cutting a big chunk from around the spine, asking us to feel how tender it is. This, he assures us, is the choicest part of the human body to eat. He passes me the knife, I begin taking meat off from everywhere, the shoulders, arms, legs. He approves, saying, “See, it is easy, just cut anywhere you want, there is no specific way.”

I find the thighs the easiest place to harvest. They have the most meat to offer. Abud Alsalam stands by as I work. I want him to have the same experience so I pass him the knife. He takes the blade, staring for a few seconds before turning his head to vomit on the floor. Looking at the mess, I ask, "What is that, sardines?"

Not saying a word, he wipes his mouth on his shoulder, beginning to finish the body. Two hours later we finish and feel experienced enough to take our knowledge back to Shatila. We wash our hands with the same bloody water, showing our teacher what we had learned by imitating his drying method on our clothes. We thank the man for sharing his expertise with us and shake his hand. He asks if we have a ride back to camp. We tell him we do not.

He graciously offers, "Then I will arrange a ride for you." He ducks back into the larger room and returns with another man. Abu Hadeed introduces him as the one who will take us home. We go upstairs to where an old dark gray Mercedes is parked. We climb in and the man turns the radio to the Revolutionary station. The radio works, but the engine will not crank. The car does not start and the man apologizes in embarrassment.

"Don't worry guys. I am going to fix you a ride."

He goes to speak with a couple of PLO soldiers that are beside an army jeep smoking and he asks them for a favor to drop us by the camp. They agree but warn us that they have to swing by a refugee school first.

"This is perfect. It is the same place that both our families are staying." Abud Alsalam tells them.

We get in the back of the jeep; the two soldiers in front. Abud

Alsalam and I sit silently during the bumpy ride as the men in the front carry on their own conversation.

Once there, we are instructed to be back in twenty minutes. The errand, we learn, is not business. They are here to visit their families too. Abud Alsalam and I enter the school, splitting up to find our respective families. My mom is looking out the window in the back room of the larger living space. Very happy to see me safe, she holds me tight for a minute and she asks if I have been eating.

"Yeah, I've been eating."

"Well, I cooked today," she informs me.

Not being one to refuse my mother's cooking, I am curious to see what she has prepared. It is fried rice with cubes of meat, I am relieved to find her so well taken care of. My brothers have been visiting and bringing my mother food more often than I am able.

I sit by her side on the mattress as she asks about the people still in the shelter and specifically about Rola. I tell her, "The people are good and Rola is the angel of the camp," explaining how she takes care of everyone. I also hint at our growing intimacy. I can tell this makes her glad, despite the sadness I see in her eyes.

After asking her repeatedly what is wrong and insisting that I must know what is troubling her; she breaks down in tears. My oldest brother, she explains, has been wounded from a rocket explosion and some of his internal organs were damaged. He was staying in Almakasad Hospital in an area called Korniesh Almazraha near the line that divides East and West Beirut. I try to comfort her telling her the hospital will take care of him

and that many people in the city are not as fortunate as he to be getting medical attention. She has been praying for him—and all of us. Perhaps, she reasons this is why he made it to a hospital. I encourage her in this, to keep praying.

I sense that my time is up although I don't have a watch. I leave my mother with another hug and a kiss on the forehead, promising that I will be fine.

The soldiers are already waiting at the jeep when I arrive and in a few more minutes Abud Alsalam also joins us. We leave our families and begin the ride back to Shatila. About seven or eight minutes into our trip we hear the walkie-talkie on one of the men go off. The man in the passenger seat turns around to tell us we have to swing by El Ramla El Badah, the White Sands beach area, to take care of an emergency situation. After changing directions, the ever-curious Abud Alsalam leans up to ask the passenger soldier what kind of emergency it is. He says, "The Israeli army is trying to take over the beach."

Looking back to me, Abud Alsalam says, "Man, we only have our nine millimeter handguns. What are we going to do?"

I can only say that we will have to try and be safe until it is over. The soldier tells the driver, "Step on the gas, drive faster, we don't want to miss the action!"

This said, the soldier driving decides to take a short cut between buildings on a one-lane street. When we have driven about midway down the street, a small green French made car comes toward us. There is no room to go around each other so the vehicles honk at each other, each wanting the other to back up. No one wants to give in and the honking continues. Soon the occupants of the small car get out with M-16s shooting into the air, attempting to intimidate us. The situation is ugly, Abud Alsalam and I are stuck in the middle.

The soldiers we ride with are in no mood to mess around. They load their AK-47s with two clips each holding thirty bullets. Two extra clips attached to these are strapped on with black duct tape for instant reloading. Not wasting any time, they open both jeep doors at once, immediately opening fire directly on the two men. I can tell these two men are surprised to become targets with no negotiation. Their surprise cannot last long as they are killed within seconds. Our soldiers shoot as they run to the car to check if there are more passengers. The tinted windows of the car give no indication. Three men in the back seat have no chance, they are sprayed with at least sixty bullets before the back doors are all the way open.

The driver returns to our jeep, the other backing the car still filled with the three dead bodies to the end of the street, allowing the jeep to pass through. The whole episode lasted only about four minutes. The first thing the passenger soldier says to us when he jumps back in is, “Thanks for all the help guys.”

Giving no answer to the absurd statement, we sit quietly; this is not our deal. Shocked at this chain of events, Abud Alsalam and I are further shocked to hear the men discuss other things, not mentioning once the violence that had just happened. While driving, the soldier expertly clicks bullets back into the empty clips. He is just as good at loading as unloading it seems.

Abud Alsalam cannot believe that we are still going to the beach; we have no choice as our chances of making it back to the camp on foot are slim.

Nearing the invasion, we see the Israeli jets overhead ejecting anti-rocket heat balloons and easily avoiding the PLO rockets. Pulling up on the beach, the soldiers dive out onto the sand on their bellies as soon as the engine is cut. The PLO lines are thick with military men and vehicles. The men all have a Rambo like appearance, black headbands, bullet chains over their chests and sweating in the heat of battle.

Only about a hundred and fifty feet separate the two armies. I cannot believe my eyes when amphibious Israeli tanks and carrier vehicles loaded with soldiers come up from the water. Most of the PLO soldiers shield themselves from assault with sand bags stacked all over the beach. Despite the technological advantage of the Israelis, the PLO positions are stronger.

Abud Alsalam and I view all this from our same back seats in the jeep. Realizing that we are not safe, we jump out running for the short cement sea wall nearby. It looks like the most likely shelter, although soldiers still fight on all sides. There is nowhere to escape, only an open expanse of road where we would surely be shot if we ran farther away.

Soon we hear three approaching Israeli helicopters that come from the horizon line. These shoot rockets in cover for their troops. At this moment the beach is transformed into hell on earth. Fire, explosions and bullets saturate the air. Twelve or more soldier loaded trucks come up from the rear, the direction we had just come, bringing reinforcements. The men unload at once, the bravest soldiers I have ever seen. Running and shooting as if they have come welcoming and expecting death. With this back-up force, the PLO is stronger and one of the helicopters is hit, turning to leave with black smoke coming from its tail. The remaining helicopters keep firing on the newly arrived soldiers. The caliber of ammunition being used by the Israeli helicopters causes men's limbs to fly everywhere. This does not stop the PLO's lines from advancing and despite the hell, I recognize that the PLO are taking control of the beach.

Suddenly, what looks like an oil drum is dropped from a roaring jet. It rolls down in slow motion as Abud Alsalam and I stand to run. The impact of this biggest explosion yet throws me twenty feet in the air and I land, crashing on the beach like a rag doll, right in the middle of the battle. I have no idea whether I am injured or not. I stay low, turning my head to see dead bodies littering the beach. This last explosion has claimed dozens of lives. This is the last card the Israeli army has against the PLO and after this they are forced to retreat as the PLO forces take control of the beach. As the Israelis retreat, three soldiers are left behind too scared to run to their vehicles. The PLO soldiers begin screaming together in one voice, "Alah Akbar, Alah Akbar! (God is great, God is great!)"

I barely hear their shouting through the pounding in my ears from the drum explosion. I stand and feel something running from my ears. I see blood covering my hand and try to wipe it away. Everyone around me is dead; I feel the luckiest of them all, cheating death once more. I run around the beach screaming for Abud Alsalam. I start going farther still screaming but realizing that my friend's hearing could be impaired too. This is the scariest moment, turning dead bodies over in the search for my best friend. Finally, I find him laying draped over a sand bag on his back, I

shake him and slap his face. He opens his eyes saying, "What happened?"

I help him up, his ears and eyes bleed, it looks like he is crying tears of blood. I tell him, "We are both alive, we are okay," wiping the blood from his face. He does the same for me, clearing away the blood from my eyes. I was unaware it was even there.

"Looks like we have something in common," he says, "we have the same injuries."

I suggest we walk to the water and wash our faces. Once finished we are like an old couple, screaming at each other as we try to hear in compensation for our injured ears.

There is a ring of PLO soldiers around the three Israeli captives. Curiously, I leave the still-bathing Abud Alsalam to see how the whole thing will end. I am shocked to hear the three Israelis begging for their lives in fluent Arabic. I assumed they would be speaking Hebrew or English, not Arabic. I wait and listen to hear them say they were pressed into service in the Israeli army against their will. They have families, children.

"Please don't kill us!" they plead, "if it were up to us we never would have come here!"

During this begging, the PLOs' flashing eyes indicate they would execute the men immediately if their higher ranking officer would allow it. Going against the will of his men the man spares their lives. I am not sure why. Perhaps he had further need of them. One PLO soldier loses control, slamming the back of his rifle into the back of one Israeli's head as hard as he can. As the prisoner drops cold the offending PLO finds the officer's gun at his head.

"If anyone tries something stupid like that again I will shoot them dead."

To cheer his men, he adds, "Look at them, they are begging for their lives like women; we do not shoot women. Besides, our orders are not to shoot prisoners."

I look next to me finding Abud Alsalam watching the scene too. It is near dusk and I tell Abud Alsalam that we need to find a new ride. The soldiers we came with are not found among the survivors.

We walk to the beach perimeter where the vehicles are parked, asking everyone if they are going to Shatila camp. One soldier in a green Land Rover truck tells us he is. When we ask for a lift he says there is plenty of room. This arranged, we jump in with some other soldiers. Abud Alsalam and I sit in the very back

The weather is beautiful; the sun is setting just over the ocean and is a blaze of fiery orange. This reminds me of how close I was to death and this in turn sends my thoughts to the only person I would be sad to leave behind. The only person that makes me happy, my girl Rola. I am lost in thoughts of her, seeing her face before me as we ride in silence back to Shatila.

Rockets still fall but this does not stop us from driving to the shelter in the heart of the camp. Right before jumping out I spot Rola standing outside the shelter waiting for my return. Quickly I get out a little angry that she is outside during an attack.

"What are you doing outside? Are you crazy standing out here while the camp is under heavy attack?"

She replies in a choked voice, "I don't care about myself. All I care about is you, and I didn't expect you to be gone all day. That made me so scared I became a nervous wreck."

Honestly, I can barely hear her. Already I feel badly for my reprimand. Knowing Rola I should have known she would be worried and waiting. I pull her into an embrace and she cries as I apologize for screaming. I wipe away her tears, explaining I just don't want her to be hurt. She sees the redness of my eyes from the pressure of the explosion, noticing next the dried blood in my ears. She screams, "What happened to you!"

I calmly reply, "A rocket exploded close to me."

I refrained from the details, not wanting to scare her.

"Well, thank God that you are okay."

Next she says a phrase I will long remember and use myself, "If something bad happens to you I will kill you!"

"That will be the best way to die."

Standing close in the empty street, I whisper, "I missed you so much," putting my hand to the side of her face.

She kisses my palm, saying, "I kiss your hand because I cannot kiss you on the lips." This is understandable but disappointing.

I ask my normal question, "How is the food supply?"

"It's okay, we have been given half a serving, so we are okay today."

I feel like we have been speaking for ten minutes or so. Meanwhile the rockets have stopped. I want to go for a walk with Rola in the beautiful weather but am hesitant because of the danger. I decide it is worth dying for and ask her to walk with me. She eagerly grabs my arm, ready and waiting to go. After a few steps down the narrow street she informs me that a sniper has been in camp all day and has killed eight people. I stop, not willing to gamble with her life. We compromise by sitting on some stairs shielded between two houses and as we sit she asks how my day was. I become quiet, not wanting to lie. She says, “I see you don’t want to talk about it. How did your school go at least?” in reference to the lesson I went to find in chopping human bodies.

I tell her, “I did chop a soldier down to skin and bones.”

She covers her mouth, grossed out.

“You really did? How did that make you feel?”

Of course I want to sound tough in front of my girl, so I brush it off, “It’s no different than cutting a cow.”

She doesn’t quite believe me, wondering how I cannot feel a difference between butchering a cow and a human. I do not want to disgust her with details. She will be eating human flesh in the near future so I end with, “Look, meat is meat.”

This makes some sense to her and she feels again that it is better not to talk more about it. I understand again why I was drawn to her in the first place. Besides her beauty she has always been able to understand me. Wanting to show concern for her day too, I ask “How was your day?”

“It was kind of sad. A woman in the shelter passed away shortly after she learned that her oldest son had been killed defending Beirut. She cried and cried until her heart stopped.”

“Poor woman,” is all I can manage.

Rola is sad as she says, “But again, it seems like we all are going to die in this war.”

I stop her, “Don’t ever say that. We’ve made it this far, we are going to make it to the end. Remember, we are going to have eight kids just like my father.”

This last part makes her smile, cheering her a little as she

confides, "Well, whatever makes you happy. I'm yours forever."

Her mother's voice screaming her name ends the conversation. Standing, she sees our heads and comes near asking Rola to come down to help clean up. Two women have become sick, vomiting in the shelter. Rola leans in close to whisper, "Must be the rats."

As she walks with her mom, she asks me, "Stay close, don't go far."

As I stand waiting I smell a barbecue. This is out of place in the starving camp. I disobey Rola's order, leaving to investigate the source of the smell. I find Abud Alsalam just down the street, approximately two-hundred feet away where he stands among six PLO fighters. They are laughing and as I near I realize they are exchanging dirty jokes. I relax, listening for a moment then ask, "What is that smell, smells like a barbecue, I just want to make sure my nose is not playing tricks on me."

The group stands near the PLO office building wall about sixty feet from the fire trying to avoid being targeted by a sniper since it is still light. One of the soldiers who is in charge of the fire runs close to turn the skewered meat, I recognize him as one of my older brother's best friends. He used to be a frequent dinner guest at our house coming to sample my mother's cooking three or four times a week. Seeing me at the same time he hugs me and kisses my cheeks while asking how my family is, wanting to hear about my brothers and my mom. I tell him of the one brother that was killed by a sniper, and the one who is recovering in the hospital.

"The rest I have not seen much of, but as far as I know they are fine. My mom is fine in her hiding refugee place."

"Well," he says, "I'm glad to hear that the majority of your brothers are okay."

Now my turn to ask after his family. He becomes quiet explaining that a rocket had hit his home three weeks earlier. It killed his mother, father, two sisters and three brothers.

"What you see is the last one standing from my family," he tells me in a casual way.

Not knowing how to reply I follow his lead, becoming quiet. Despite his light treatment of the subject I know he is only behaving with so little emotion because this is the mandatory attitude we have all grown up with. Trying to guide the conversation to less sensitive areas, I ask, "Where have you guys been getting this meat from?"

All the men laugh at my question, except the serious Abud Alsalam. My friend points to a body lying a ways off between two houses. Walking closer to see, I find a naked man's body with his thighs, calves, and shoulders carved out. I learn that this is the sixth body the men have eaten from in the last four days having harvested only the meatiest parts as there is no lack in the supply. I thought that I was the pioneer in Shatila for this necessity, but then again the process is not an original invention. Returning to the group, I feel sheepish for thinking that only I have thought seriously of eating human flesh since the announcement on TV. Looking to read Abud Alsalam's eyes, he knows my thoughts exactly and smiles knowingly as I stop short the funny comment I feel he is about to say. It is clear to me that human steak is cooking on the open half-barrel barbecue grill. My brother's soldier friend asks, "What did you think we would be barbecuing?"

"I had no idea, that is why I asked."

"Have you eaten human flesh yet?"

"Not yet, but tomorrow is supposed to be the day."

He puts another question to me, "How hungry are you?"

"I'm really hungry."

"Then you are going to eat it and you are going to be happy about it. I have been eating it for four days now. Once it is cooked I can't tell the difference."

I feel he is trying to initiate me to the experience cheerfully and I appreciate the gesture. I don't know if this is a step up or a step down from eating cats and dogs.

Soon a soldier comes carrying a silver tray loaded with small cubes of human shish-ka-bob setting it on the steps next to us. The meat is grabbed on all sides with no hesitation. The soldiers eat the hot meat immediately while their conversation continues uninterrupted. Abud Alsalam and I take the cue from the men; perhaps this is not such a big deal. Needing no invitation and at the same time we each take hold of a stick. Still hesitant to take the first bite, one of the guys notices, encouraging us with, "Hey guys you have to eat it while it's still hot, otherwise it will get chewy and you will really taste it when it cools. If you guys are going to eat, this is the time."

This makes sense so I lift the stick to my nose, testing it. It smells delicious, whether because I am very hungry or because it is actually good I do not know. Either way, I must get used to the taste and the idea; I have to try what I will be feeding to the others in the shelter first. I have no choice anyway, this is the only food we will have from this moment on. I sink my teeth into the first cube, slowly starting to chew, wanting get the taste of it. This may be a bad idea. The meat is not meant to be enjoyed, only to stave off hunger. Better to chew hurriedly and swallow, respecting the sacrifice of the people that are keeping us alive through their death. The texture is tough. The juice like brine; too salty, crunching between my teeth and under my tongue. No spices or salt have been added. The taste is inherent in the flesh itself. As I swallow the first bite, the aftertaste is sour like lemon. I ask to make sure, "Did you guys add any spice or lemon to this?"

They laugh again, "There is no lemon in the whole camp. What you are tasting is real. This is what the human flesh tastes like."

The only comparable aspect between beef and human meat is its raw appearance. The flavors are foreign to each other. I have never tasted any kind of meat even close to this. I remember Abud Alsalam who has been watching me go first, seeing him still holding his uneaten stick. I tell him, "Go ahead and eat it, it is not that bad at all."

He still hesitates. I understand, this is a difficult concept to get through. The PLO guys are watching Abud Alsalam debate internally whether to eat or not. I lean in to whisper, "You have to eat it brother. You are going to look weak in front of those natural born killers."

With his manhood on the line, the debate turns into a challenge, or at least I make it sound this way to push him over the edge. This said, he shoves two cubes, not one, into his mouth, chewing furiously and finishing the whole stick quickly. I am shocked and surprised to see him go for seconds, grabbing another stick from the tray.

The soldiers' attention turns back to their jokes. Abud Alsalam and I are relieved that our mission is accomplished. Our first human flesh eating experience now behind us. Dinner now over, the conversation becomes heated as politics and bravery come up. One of the soldiers tells a story from the night before. He and a few other men had crossed behind enemy lines and engaged the invaders; two Israeli soldiers were killed, four others wounded. He relates the tale proudly, waving his hands as he speaks excitedly as the men pat him on the back in approval. Trying to top this, another soldier tells us how he had made a direct hit on an Israeli tank with an anti-tank launcher, an RBJ He finishes on a sad note admitting the mission was not complete without the annihilation of the tank's crew, who were rescued by a fighter helicopter. Then again, he mentions, although the mission was not a complete success, it was fun to take a shot at the enemy.

I enjoyed hearing the stories from outside the camp. One of the soldier's attention turns to me, "When are you going to join us to go to the real war?"

"When the Israeli army attacks my camp, then that will leave me no choice but to defend the camp that I grew up in. Until then, I am out of this war."

Not wanting to sound cowardly I go on to explain about my responsibilities of feeding and protecting the shelter people. He seems to understand my point, his curiosity abated for now. Immediately after this a bullet hits the metal fire barrel with a loud bang, we jump in concert, backing away to the safety of the PLO office behind us. One soldier bravely runs to cover the barrel with a lid, smothering the light source to protect any passers by on the street. While inside the office, a candle is lit. As we seat ourselves on the cement floor away from the windows, our conversation continues on the same subject—politics. I see the guys have begun to argue back and forth and I lose interest, deciding to leave and check on Rola, who is ever-present in the back of my mind. Before going I ask Abud Alsalam if he wants to join me but he is enjoying the talk more than I so I leave him to it.

Under the cover of darkness I run zigzagging down the street still mindful of the sniper. I arrive quickly covering the short distance to the shelter safely. It is late, about one thirty in the morning, but I have a feeling that Rola is still awake. My eyes search for her by the light of a few lit candles and I find her on the mattress next to her mother, laying on her side listening to a small transistor radio. I gingerly walk through the room full of slumbering people, finally getting to her mattress near the wall. I have done a good job of being quiet, she does not notice me until I am very near, gasping in surprise when she looks up. I will never forget the sparkle of happiness in her eyes in that candle light. She is happy to see me. Of course I feel I am in the choicest place in the universe, my heart pounds just looking at her. I could look at her face until the end of my life—this could be any second so I take advantage of the time I have.

Rola leans toward me as I sit next to her on the floor, blowing out the candle next to her. With the room much darker now, Rola does a shocking thing; she kisses me barely on the lips, just enough to make a sound. I am taken aback by her boldness. Her mother sleeps facing us on the mattress; this move is a great risk on her part. I am not complaining. There are butterflies in my stomach,

like the rush of a roller-coaster ride. This is my first kiss ever from any girl. Even as I experience the moment I think of not only her mother, but the room full of people who could be witnessing our exchange. My identity fades in the euphoria, I have just died and gone to heaven. As she pulls her head away from the kiss, I open my eyes to catch her gaze just visible in the low light, I want to see more of this woman. I retrieve the lighter from my pocket to light the same candle she just blew out. We look at each other for a few minutes quietly, only conversing with our eyes. It being late, I think it kind to leave her to sleep, not wanting to selfishly keep her up. Standing to go, she moves to stop me, demanding in an intense whisper, "No!" while grabbing my hand, trying to push me back down to the floor.

I kneel, whispering back, "You need to get some rest, I know you wake up early."

"I don't care, I want you to stay."

Her mother surprises both of us, opening her eyes to add, "Please, stay for the love of God so I can sleep."

I have a deep respect for Rola's mother, feeling ashamed that I have caused her to wake up. Rola and I smile, laughing softly at the turn of events. In our hushed laughter we keep whispering, trying not to wake the whole room. Upon her insistence I lay down on the cement next to her bed. She offers to find me a blanket but I do not want her to stir and wake her mother again, assuring her I am fine as we lay holding hands. She reveals her heart to me; I am driving her crazy. She cannot stop thinking about me, wondering about my safety, she hates our separations even if only for a few minutes. While hearing her confessions I realize

it is a mirror of my own feelings but I do not want to parrot these things back to her exactly; I decide to hold back. If I open my mouth I can only repeat her words.

I turn my feelings down a different avenue, vowing that I will replace the loss of her father and brothers. I will be her best friend, taking good care of her and her mother as long as I live. I know already that I will fulfill my first promise. Once this war is over I will be the best husband that I can be to this most beautiful angel. I have no choice in this, she is the only kindness I find among the ugly cruelty of this life. As she listens to this I see her sadness grow with tears threatening, her head sinks in hiding to her arm. Not knowing the nature of her tears I am concerned; I know how sensitive Rola is and begin to worry that I have offended her in some way. Asking if this is true, if I have offended her, she stops me, saying, "No, this is the most beautiful thing you could have said to me."

Unexpectedly I hear a cry coming from behind Rola. Her mother is obviously touched by our conversation as well, she holds her hand to her face as she rolls away, crying behind us for several minutes. This is all embarrassing, for twenty minutes straight Rola and I look at each other while listening to the sobs of her mother that have given away her audience to our whispers. Eventually her mother half-rises while wiping her tears, saying to me directly, "Your mom has the sweetest heart in the whole camp and your father is a true hero. No one can deny his sacrifices here; he did a lot of goodness using his power as a religious man, using the strength of eight sons who are willing to die in the people's defense. The day you ask for my daughter's hand in marriage, that

will be her biggest honor. You are no less a hero than the rest of your family. I want you to know, when you do ask for her hand, my answer in advance is yes, you have my blessing. You can call me Mom."

This said, she rolls over, turning her back to us. Unwilling to take another chance in not knowing if she is still listening, I lay on the cement, rest my head on my arm and fall asleep watching Rola's eyes.

I wake up hearing the people stirring, clothes rustling, children playing. It is around seven in the morning, knowing it is still early from the tiredness of my eyes. I try to move, feeling the excruciating pain from my cold side. My neck, shoulder and side, all the way down to my foot are all ice from my few hours of sleeping on the cement. Adjusting and moving my back from side to side, it takes me a while to allow the blood to circulate back into my limbs. Struggling, I manage to stand, looking back at the peacefully sleeping Rola. I walk slowly away, hoping she will continue in her rest. I leave the basement and walk back to the PLO office in search of Abud Alsalam. I see the soldiers sleeping everywhere and pick my way through them to my friend. Once found I poke him twice in the shoulder. He opens one eye, looking up at me from his curled sleeping position saying, "Just give me one more hour, please."

Not willing to do so, I lean down closely to whisper, "We have a job to do."

Now opening both eyes with some anger, he says, "I did not sign up for this, to be awakened so early in the morning!"

I encourage him, "Come on man, these people in the shelter

need us, they depend on us to bring them food! We can't help them if you stay asleep."

This touches him a little; he sits up rubbing his eyes saying, "Okay, okay, I get your point."

He grabs his handgun, holstering it in the back of his pants as he slowly stands. He and I step over the men to get to the door. Once out, I tell him, "Well, we will be needing a big kitchen knife."

He is still bitter about the early morning wake up. "Couldn't you find the kitchen knife before you woke me up?"

I ignore the question, saying, "Okay, let's go search the houses for the biggest knife we can find."

In the fourth house we are pleased to find a heavy duty twelve-inch butcher knife. This is the best blade for the job. We wrap the object with a towel, precaution necessary with this sharp blade. As we begin the first fresh body hunt, Abud Alsalam wonders aloud, "How are we going to tell which body is fresh and which is not?"

"Well," I say, "this is a good question as they all look the same to me."

He then suggests, "Let's smell it. If it smells bad we will leave it alone."

This seems a good idea to me, so we walk the length of the street sniffing each body as we go, taking our chances with the possibility of snipers. All the bodies smell bad. The morning heat has turned the bodies alive only yesterday a greenish unattractive color. Out of ideas and not agreeing on a single body to begin with, we walk faster, looking for skin tint instead of relying on smell.

We come upon a soldier in full uniform who is weakly raising his right arm. Laying in a pool of his own blood with an AK-47 at his side, bullet wounds in his trachea and just above his left eye indicate he has no chance of survival. His whole face is bloody, the eye below the shot almost black with internal bleeding. We can only assume a sniper got the best of him. We stand looking down on him, he seems young, about our age, we cannot be sure from the blood. This does not keep Abud Alsalam from being discreet as he leans in to say, "He is fresh meat."

I turn my head sharply, saying, "Stop it."

Abud Alsalam grabs me by the shirt, pulling me away six or seven feet from the dying soldier, "Look, we are searching for fresh meat." Pointing at the dying man, "Here we have found it. Why are we arguing?"

Feeling that Abud Alsalam has a point I realize my emotions had overcome my logic. While we talk, the soldier begins to seize; shaking and kicking his feet. We take this as a sign he is nearing the end and step aside to take shelter next to a house not wanting to be another target for the same sniper. We watch from this vantage, it is not long before he stops moving completely. Walking back to the scene, I kneel down next to his body asking Abud Alsalam to unroll the knife and give me the towel. I cannot help myself, I must see the face of this brave soldier. I wipe the coagulated blood from his face just enough to recognize his features. Looking up I scream, "This is Zaid Deyab!"

He was our classmate in high school.

"Oh no!"

I ask Abud Alsalam, "What are we going to do?"

I see that he is as sad as I, knowing this is one of our longtime friends. Abud Alsalam says, "There is nothing we could have done with no hospitals and no medicine. He was going to die regardless. We can stand here most likely to be shot just like him, or we can carry him to one of those safe houses and chop him up. At least we know the guy."

"At least we know the guy? What, is that supposed to make me feel better?"

"No, I'm not trying to make you feel better, but I promise you that he doesn't mind being chopped now."

I tell Abud Alsalam, who is poorly trying to prove his point, "Well what are you trying to say? I know you are trying to make a point, but you are not making it."

"I am just trying to make you feel better."

"Well, you are not doing a good job at it."

He says, "You are the one who came to the room to wake me up. You are the one who brought me here to find a fresh body—and now we have. Are we going to chop him or not?"

He puts me on the spot. I struggle, thinking it would not be so hard if I did not know the guy. I scream as loud as I can in frustration.

"Okay, okay, let's do this!"

I do not think I have won the argument. The issue is not about us, it is about the hungry people. While we stand arguing I see other people searching among the bodies. They are on similar missions. This gives me confidence and the urgency I need to know this is the right thing to do. Right away we each take hold of a hand, dragging the body across the street to a vacant house,

not wanting to skin the man in the street. We move a coffee table away from the center of the rug in the living room, clearing enough space for our work. Placing the body in the middle of the room, Abud Alsalam begins to strip the body of clothes, when he comes to the underwear I yell, "Leave that alone, let's not take his dignity and pride away!"

Still feeling sad, Abud Alsalam notices this in my eyes, "You don't have to do anything. I can do the whole job by myself. If you feel bad you can step outside, I will call you when I'm done."

"It's not about that."

"Okay do you want us to go look for a different body? Would that make you feel better?"

I feel my eyes begin to brim, a few seconds more and I will be crying. I walk outside, leaving Abud Alsalam with the body. I need to pull myself together. I feel I am losing control. Once outside I look at the sky thinking to myself why God is doing this to us; where is the justice? Thinking how hard this is, me being just a teenager, having to skin and chop a friend to feed others. I am full of anger not knowing who to blame. Do I blame God or myself, for this shit hole that I was born in. All I know is the anger, wanting to scream as hard as I can. Finally with no premeditation, I keep my eyes on the sky saying, "I shall never pray to you as long as I live."

From this moment on I know that I have lost my faith. Despite my religious upbringing, I do not know if my faith will ever be restored.

I light a cigarette to calm myself, watching the other people finding bodies as I smoke. It is good to know that Abud Alsalam and I are not the only brave ones in this mess. These people are not being as particular about the selection process. I worry, hoping that disease will not spread among the people. Punctuating this thought by throwing my half-smoked cigarette away, I return to the living room to see Abud Alsalam busy working. He carves the thigh meat away from the bone with the knife. Looking at the body I notice it is headless. I ask, "Where is the head?" even as my eyes search the room for it.

"I put it in the kitchen sink."

I have to ask why.

"Well, I did not want him to keep staring at me as I cut his body."

"You could have closed his eyes."

"Believe me I would still feel his eyes even if they were closed shut."

I ask him to take a break, feeling this is best as he seems to be at an emotional breaking point. Without hesitation he stands handing me the bloody knife, both his arms to the elbows are dripping with blood. I tell him as I put the lighter and cigarette pack on the floor, "Go find something in the house to clean your hands with so you can have a cigarette break."

"Sure, I am in immediate need of a cigarette."

I turn my attention to the body, beginning to work on the second thigh. Making my way up to the shoulders, I remember the lesson from Burg-el Barajneh camp as I turn the body on its stomach, cutting the tender meat shanks from around the spine. I pile all the meat on the rug next to me, moving back to the lower body again, cutting the calves away. I clean away all the usable meat and by the time I finish the body is a virtual skeleton. The

house is steaming in the summer heat, I feel the sweat dripping from my face and nose onto my pants. Abud Alsalam walks back in from his long, long cigarette break. I pass him the knife, asking him to chop a large chunk of meat into smaller pieces. I rise from my sitting position on the rug, walking the circle of the room while watching Abud Alsalam finish the job. I see that my friend is heaving, nauseated and hacking, almost ready to vomit as he cuts the meat in the hot room. I ask him, "Are you okay, do you want me to take over again?"

"No, it's not the body, it's the heat."

Even though I doubt this, I do not want to expose him. I empathetically agree, "Yeah, it's pretty hot in here."

He works fast, it does not take him long to complete chopping the thirty to thirty-five pounds of pure meat. We wrap the fresh meat in a clean green bed sheet we find folded neatly in a closet next to the bed. I take another of the sheets to clean my hands, they are still sticky from the blood and it's the best I can do with no water. Abud Alsalam follows my example and once done he slings the load on his back. We head down the street to the shelter, the bed sheet dripping blood on Abud Alsalam's army shirt, trailing a line of red drops on the asphalt as we walk. He comments on the way, "I think we will never go hungry ever again."

I have to agree with him.

We share the burden as we go, switching the heavy meat back and forth between us until we arrive. I go down the shelter stairs with the meat straight back to where a kitchen is separated by blankets from the rest of the room. I lay the sheet full of meat on the floor, seeing the same tough woman who helped butcher the rats. I stick my head and arm out from the blanket screen, waving her to come discreetly, not wanting Rola to notice my unkempt presence. My whole backside is soaked in blood and I want to spare her the sight if possible. After a few waves I succeed in summoning the woman. I close the blankets behind the woman and Abud Alsalam, who is right behind her. I show the meat in the bed sheet to her, she asks the expected question, "Where did you get this meat?"

Abud Alsalam replies right away, "It's horse meat."

I think this is a smart reply, the woman surprises us with, "We don't eat horses."

I feel a history lesson is called for to make her feel better.

"Well, in the Islamic religion you can eat horses. It is not prohibited. Plus, our great, great grandfathers ate horses on a daily basis."

It is her turn to be surprised as I convince her with a true historical story about a man and his horse.

The man, Hatam El-taee who was famous for being one of the most generous men in the Middle East, had one of the most beautiful Arabian horses to be found. One of the rival kings offered him fifty-thousand gold denar, a vast sum, as payment if he would sell the horse. Hatam El-taee refused, even though he was poor and living in a one bedroom house with his wife and had no furniture except a rag and a few pillows.

One day around eleven at night a family of five knocks on his door, tired and starving of hunger from long desert travel. He welcomes them in, asking his wife if they had anything for the family to eat.

"We have nothing, not even dry bread," she says.

Hatam El-taee goes behind the house and slaughters his horse for the sake of being a good host. His wife then cooks some of the meat to feed the hungry guests.

I tell this true story for two purposes, one to cover for my friend, and two, to convince this woman who I know for a fact can convince everyone else in the shelter to eat the meat. I kill two birds with one stone.

The woman is totally won over. I give her a chance to arrange the meat and she begins separating it into piles. While she works I peek my head out of the blankets again to search for Rola. I find her sitting on the mattress but I cannot tell what she is doing. Too late to hide, my eyes contact hers. I wonder why she does not come to see me, something is wrong. Curious to know what is going on I excuse myself from the kitchen, leaving Abud Alsalam speaking with the woman. I walk toward Rola no longer caring about my appearance, my only concern is why she does not seem happy to see me. Stopping two feet from where she sits, I ask, "What is wrong?"

"I am just scared to look at the meat."

"Is that all?" I ask. "I was thinking you might be mad at me."

"Why would I be mad at you. I just don't think that I can eat this meat."

"Why not? I thought we talked about this before." I continue with, "I tried it last night and believe me, it's not as bad as you think. It's just meat like any other meat."

Her voice changes pitches, "Still, it's a human!"

"Hey, lower your voice before somebody hears you."

"It's okay, I think everyone here knows about the human meat. They have been talking about it all day."

"Well it doesn't matter, but don't you say anything to anybody, especially that woman, we told her it is horse meat."

"Okay, I won't tell. I promise."

CHAPTER THREE

A Sniper's Bullet

August 16, 1982. The day begins quietly; no rockets are falling, which is unusual. No one complains of this. We are accustomed to sleeping and waking with explosions. This temperate peaceful day encourages the people of both Sabra and Shatila camps to come out of their shelters to enjoy the balmy summer morning. They are out in force taking short walks, stretching their sore limbs from sitting in hiding too long.

Some go to check their homes, not having been back since the start of the invasion over two months before. I have not seen this many live people on the streets at once for such a long time. I enjoy watching the peaceful day, or what looked like it. This brief dangerous peace gives the PLO soldiers an opportunity to make food runs to the starving camps. Three trucks loaded with hundred-pound burlap sacks of rice and dates all stamped with "PRODUCT OF IRAQ" park in the main street of Shatila. The foodstuff, one of the soldiers tells me, has been donated by the country of Iraq to the people of Beirut.

Abud Alsalam and I are happily compelled to unload the trucks carrying one heavy bag at a time on our backs to the shelter and other homes. Some residents still refuse to go underground, preferring the danger of their own homes. We know that now food hunts will not be necessary for a long time. The labor is welcome.

During a break, I comment, "What a wonderful day; it's quiet, no rockets falling, nice weather, now food."

We do not think it can be any better, even so we feel it is too good to be true, hoping there is no trick behind the silence of the skies. After exchanging these comments, my friend and I continue to unload along side the soldiers until the last bag is off the truck. Our backs are aching from the work and Abud Alsalam suggests a pleasure walk, taking some time for ourselves to stretch our backs. It is a chance to walk without fear, we assume the peace will last a few more hours. Not having any assurance this is true we set off in great hope.

The sun sets as Abud Alsalam and I wander in the narrow alleys between houses. The weather is so gorgeous, the sun a hanging chandelier, glowing bright orange in the sky. The only mar on the otherwise perfect moment is the awful stench emanating from the exposed human bodies on the street. Even being used to the smell, I always hope that it will go away; it is the only thing that cannot be imagined away. Abud Alsalam and

I walk side by side. He is at my right hand, annoyingly kicking a small stone as he concentrates on telling me his dreams for the future. Not wanting to break his thoughts, I resist telling him to stop with the stone. He goes on about rebuilding the family furniture store bigger than before, letting his father retire as he takes over the business. I think the simple dream is attainable, I tell him. Starting small and reconstructing on the burned site there is no reason why this cannot be.

"Yeah, I know it's not that big of a dream." Abud Alsalam replies.

He tells me again the familiar story of how hard his father worked to make the store grow. I listen out of respect, knowing the tale well.

Still walking, he turns the question on me, asking, "What about you? What is your dream?"

Wanting to be brief, I answer, "You know what my dream is."

He knows me as well as I know myself and he understands, "To marry Rola?"

"Yes, plus go to college, make something of myself if I survive this war."

"That is a simple dream, I think you will marry Rola and go to college. You were always the smartest one of us. I have no doubt you are going to make it to college. As far as this war, we have made it this far, I think we will be lucky enough to make it to the end."

It is good to hear the confidence my friend has in me professed out loud.

Still speaking, I see a single line of red fluid spray diagonally down the front of my green military shirt, from my right shoulder to my left. I exclaim, "What is that!"

Abud Alsalam pushes my shoulder forcefully with both hands toward cover between two houses then he throws himself in the alley opposite of mine. A six foot gap, the width of the street, separates he and I. I am still dumbly standing on my side of the alley when he screams to me, "Duck down!"

I still do not know what is going on but hearing the urgency in his voice I sit down, leaning my back against the side of a painted yellow house. Abud Alsalam says in a calm voice, "I am hit." He opens the first three buttons of his shirt to reveal a large chest wound. I see as he turns to show me that the hole in the middle of his chest is the size of a quarter.

"I guess I have to forget about the furniture store."

At hearing him say this, I feel hot tears dropping from both my cheeks. I scream at him, "No, no, not you!"

"Why not, did you think that I was going to survive?"

In my heart I knew there was no answer I could give. It was too late. I had to be next to him so I stood, intending to jump to his side. It was his turn to scream, "What are you doing! Sit your ass down!"

Seeing in my eyes that I am coming to him regardless, he began to plead, "Please, stay on your side. The sniper is experienced. He is not playing around. Please stay on your side."

I test the air past the screen of the building with my hand, holding it out twelve or thirteen seconds to see if the sniper is still waiting. A bullet whizzes one inch from the top of my thumb, lodging in the wall behind me.

I see that Abud Alsalam grows weaker, still he is concerned for me, saying, “Please stay on your side, don’t get yourself killed too.”

I stand looking, seeing blood drip down his mouth to his chest. I say, “Try not to talk, save your strength.”

“Why not talk? We both know I am going to die anyway.”

I see he is struggling to keep his eyes open, I begin crying in earnest, like a baby. I decide to cross to his side no matter what, giving the sniper a chance to shoot me. I scream, “You are not dying alone today!”

I walk slowly two or three steps as a bullet ricochets off the button on my shirt and enters my right bicep, splitting the button on its journey. It looks like the sniper miscalculated my speed, I do not care, feeling nothing will stop me from reaching my best friend. I make it across with minimal damage, the sniper loses the only shot he had. I sit next to Abud Alsalam.

“You must be so crazy, risking your life like that. You didn’t think of Rola, you didn’t think of your family?”

“I didn’t think of anything, I just wanted to be with you.”

“You could have got yourself killed.”

“Look at me, I’m okay. Look at you!”

“I told you, you are very lucky. Even when you give the sniper a good shot he only gets a button and your arm. Even as we were walking, he chose to shoot me. I’m glad he did.”

“He should have shot me. It looks like he has crossed eyes.”

Abud Alsalam tries to smile, the blood runs more freely from his mouth as he does. I grab the pack from my back pocket, lighting two cigarettes. I place one between his fingers, joking, “Well, they say that cigarettes will kill you.”

I feel that now he is too weak to smile. He asks me, "Tell my mom to be strong. Tell her I am sorry," he pauses for a few seconds as tears flow from his closed eyes, "Remember when we were little kids in the third grade?"

"Yes, I remember, what are you referring to?"

My friend cannot finish the sentence. This is the last thing he says, his head falls to rest on his shoulder. Just like that my long life friend is gone. His blood pools under him, my side touches his, soaking the pants of my right thigh.

Raising my hand to touch his face, I see blood running down my elbow from the bullet. Taking the six-click knife out, I open the wound further digging for the bullet. I squeeze the blood from above the wound, trying to force out any contamination. After a few tries I succeed in the surgery, removing the bullet that has fortunately only entered the flesh.

I am numb emotionally as well as physically. I feel almost no pain. Reaching over to unbuckle the belt I know Abud Alsalam always wears, I tighten it around my upper arm to slow the flow of blood.

Not willing to leave my best friend yet, I find myself talking to him about everything I can think of for the next two hours non-stop. For some reason I feel he hears me, that he is listening. I continue until it is completely dark, I can feel the numbness of my tied arm. My finger tips are yellow, my hand moves with difficulty; it is time to go. My feet are willing but my heart is not.

I stand in the darkness barely seeing my friend's form. Striking my lighter, I take with me one last look at his face. I kneel in his blood, kissing his forehead once as I hug him a minute or two,

whispering in his ear, "I love you so much, I will never forget you. You will always be in my heart and my mind."

Standing again from the farewell, I say, "If I could carry you on my shoulder I would, I will be back to get you for a proper burial. I am not going to leave you rotting on the street. This I promise."

Walking back in the narrow streets, I cry for the terrible loss of my best friend.

Passing the PLO office where we had the barbecue not long ago, I find two soldiers outside smoking. Coming near, the soldier who is my brother's best friend stops me when he sees the belt on my arm. He pulls me aside into the office lit by three candles and sitting me in a chair he says, "I see you are shot, first I have to take the bullet out."

"I already did."

"You did it yourself?"

"Yes."

"How long has it been since you tied it?"

"About two hours."

"That is dangerous, you can't cut the blood flow from your arm for two hours. You could lose this arm."

I do not reply as he opens the tie on a military knapsack and pulls out a small white plastic bottle. He opens it and pours the clear liquid directly into my wound. White foam forms, I grasp my left knee so hard from the sting of the liquid that it bruises. Now putting a handful of loose cotton against my arm, he wraps white cloth followed with silver duct tape to secure the dressing. Warmth creeps back into my arm, blood rushes back through my veins. I ask him, "Are we done?"

"Yes, this is the best we can do but I think you are going to be fine."

I stand to walk away and he stops me. "Why all this sadness in your eyes?"

Not willing to talk about it, I choose to answer with silence.

"Somebody died?"

Again I am quiet.

"Okay, you are going to walk with all the blood on your clothes?"

From the same bag he takes out a set of military clothes placing them on the chair I just rose from.

"They are not clean I wore them before, but at least they are not bloody."

I remove my shoes, pants and shirt; blood still wet on the skin of my thigh.

"Don't put the clothes on yet."

He steps out, returning with a gallon jug partially full of water, telling me to clean myself before dressing. Using the unsoiled parts of what I just took off, I wash the blood from my arm and thigh before I gratefully put the new clothes on.

I am pleased that the shirt is long sleeved, it covers my wound well. He passes the jug back to me as I button the cuffs, saying, "Here, drink as much as you can. You lost a lot of blood, you need more fluid in your system."

I drink as much as possible asking, "If it's not too much, can I get enough to wash my face?"

"What, you think you are the prince of England? There is no water in the camp, do you know how hard it was to get that much?"

Even so, he says, “Yes, open your hands,” as he pours a little into my hands. It is wonderful to freshen up; I rub my face, bringing the rest to wash my hair and neck. Turning as I leave, I thank him for what he did.

“You are welcome.”

He asks once more curiously, “You are shot in the arm yet your thigh and backside are full of blood, how is that?”

I give him a half-smile, walking away to the shelter.

In the darkness on the way I stop to lean against a wall, overwhelmed by complete emptiness. I have not only lost my best friend, I have lost hope. With Abud Alsalam gone, the whole word is coming to an end. Paramount of these swirling thoughts is the insistent question of why the sniper chose him, not me. The gunman had a clear shot of us both, equally at his mercy. I wonder about the sniper, the technicality of the shot he chose in the positions where Abud Alsalam and I had stood; I was the more logical choice, at least this is what I am thinking. Perhaps I think these things because I want to be the one who was shot. I would trade places with my friend in a heartbeat if it were up to me. Unfortunately this was up to one person, the sniper, and he made his choice. I still think he made the wrong one.

I replay the slow steps I took between the buildings, giving the man a deliberate chance to take my life. How could he have missed me?

I force my feet forward the rest of the short distance to the shelter. Downstairs I go to find the only person able to comfort me, Rola. She sits in a circle of children, reading a story to them by candle light. She sees me. Our eyes connect as I go towards the privacy of the screened kitchen space; within seconds she is with me.

"You don't look good. Your face is yellow."

I think my appearance reflects the quantity of blood I lost from my arm.

"Something happened?"

As much as I hate to let her see any weakness in me, not able to possess myself, I break, dropping to my knees crying. She feels the seriousness of my grief, her eyes are scared. Coming down to my level, she kneels, "Please tell me, what is wrong?"

I can barely speak. The emotional pressure is too great. I manage, "They killed Abud Alsalam."

Tears roll down her cheeks to mingle with mine. She knows the closeness of our friendship; he is the only one who can finish my thoughts.

We sit quietly for five minutes on the kitchen floor, no words, not even from Rola, can be of any help. All my mind can contain now is the cold reality that I am alone, that I am guilty in not sharing his fate. The depth of this fresh sorrow sinks deeper than any I have known, even the loss of my brother was not as scathing as this wrenching injustice. I always knew he was closer to me than my own blood.

Sitting privately with Rola, this is the first that I have been unable to feel her presence; truly I am alone. I stand, moving the blankets to leave. Rola runs to stop me, asking, "Where are you going?"

"I have to inform his family."

"How will you get there? It's a long way."

"I don't know how I'm going to get there, but I will get there."

She knows she cannot stop me from going. She can only watch as I climb the stairs. Walking down the dark street, my purpose is firm. I will make it there even if I am killed trying.

To leave the camp I must pass near to where Abud Alsalam's body lay, I swing by to see him, finding him in the same position. This time avoiding his blood, I sink down to his level, touching his face as I do. The hot summer night has not kept the coldness of death from his skin. I tell him, "I am sorry I left you here alone, believe me, I feel alone even though I am still alive. No amount of crying will satisfy the sorrow that you leave behind. All our lives we did the same things at the same time, only sleep separated us. Each next morning we would wake up and do it all over again. I am sorry we had to live a life like the one we have lived, the way we had to grow up. Even though we are only eighteen years old, we have the experience of a forty-year old man not in life, but in death."

I apologize again that we had to grow up so fast.

"Then again, even though you are gone there is nothing you will miss out on in this life; there is only death, death and more death. Don't feel bad. It is only a matter of time before I join you."

I reach behind his back for the gun that barely hangs from his pants, I already took the belt that always secured it for my wounded arm. Abud Alsalam's pants are always baggy, handed down as custom by his brothers; the belt is a staple, a trademark.

The tip of the gun's barrel is bloody, I take a closer look with my lighter to see, attempting to wipe it on Abud Alsalam's shoulder. The blood is dry. Opening the chamber, I see a bullet waiting, loaded and ready to be shot. Gun in hand, I get a crazy idea: *if it is only a matter of time until I join him, why not now?* The heaviness of the gun weight in my hand mirrors my thoughts. Even though the idea is tempting, the easiest way out, the only thing staying my hand is the promises I made Rola. I not only promised to marry her, but also I promised to look after she and her mother. I wipe the idea from my mind with more success than the blood from the gun. I replace it in Abud Alsalam's pants and I promise him, "I'm going to go right now to inform your family. If I make it alive, I will be back to give you a proper burial."

I lean down, kissing both his cheeks before leaving. Rockets are falling in distant Beirut and the fires are visible from the street I walk on. I wonder why tonight the camp is spared.

Over an hour I walk the deserted roads. I am thinking it is two, two-thirty in the morning when I begin to black out, dizzy and faint. My last meal was too long ago and I feel weakness from the blood lost earlier in the day. Staggering drunkenly, I see a vehicle light coming toward me from behind at high speed. My shadow shoots out in front, the light's brightness growing quickly. I turn, arms open wide in the middle of the street, not caring if they stop or run me over. The driver hits the brakes so hard he almost loses control, fish-tailing, finally stopping five or six feet from me. The driver sticks his head from the window, cursing as he asks, "What are you suicidal? If you are there are a million ways you can do it besides this."

The passenger also sticks himself out the window, adding, "Move your ass, we are on a mission, we have a wounded person in the back."

The light blinds my eyes so that I cannot make out the kind of vehicle I have stopped, I move to the driver's side and see a large red cross painted on the white side, an ambulance. I ask the driver, "Where you guys going?"

"We are going to the Burj-El Mor area."

This is close to the school where I am headed.

"Do you guys mind giving me a lift?"

"Well, we are not a taxi."

"It's on your way."

"No, this vehicle is for injured people only."

I reach for my hand gun and put it to his head, "You are right, someone is going to be injured."

"Please don't shoot, we are unarmed people. Get in the back with the injured people."

"Get out and open the back door for me."

"Don't you trust me?"

"No, I don't."

At this the passenger opens his door, walking with me to the rear where he opens the door to let me climb in. Immediately I make my way to the end of the cargo space, close enough to the men in the cab to keep my gun on them, making sure they don't try anything. We drive away and I see from the red interior lights that the injured people are not alive, they are a greenish color. I estimate from my experience that they are three or four days dead.

Leaning against the metal net separating us, I yell, "You bastards, I thought you said you are carrying injured people!"

"Well, they make us work all day long, we drive around all day with these dead people. Do you know how many injured people are in this city? Hundreds if not thousands. If we pick them up, where will we take them? The two hospitals are filled and overflowing."

"You know what I would like to do, I would like to shoot both of you, right here right now."

"Please don't shoot us, I know what we are doing is wrong, but there is nothing else we can do."

"So you are letting those injured people in the camps and city die, knowing that you could help them? Just take them to the hospital, put them in the lobby on the floors. Let the hospital take the responsibility of them. You two clowns are messing with people's lives."

The driver bites back sarcastically, "What, you think you are Mother Theresa?"

I shoot two bullets in the windshield, the holes stare back through the broken glass, the driver screams, "Sorry, sorry!"

"I wonder, If I shoot your knee caps right now, would you get medical attention?"

"Please don't do it!"

"Answer the question."

"Yeah, I think so."

"Then you *can* get people medical attention. If you pick up an injured person off the street then you can take them to the hospital. You can get them the same medical attention you would get."

He was silent. I notice then that there are several Bounty candy bars in the ash tray and a bottle of apple juice between them in the consul. Grabbing at them automatically, I reach through to get a candy bar, but the driver stops me when I go for the juice, telling

me, "No, no. I'll give you a full one," as he pulls an unopened container from a whole case kept under his seat.

Seizing and opening the bottle, I down half, stopping only to eat the coconut chocolate candy. I chase this with the remaining juice, commenting, "Well, looks like my lucky day; I got a ride and a dinner."

The closer we got to my destination, the closer together the rockets are falling on all sides. The passenger turns to me, pleading, "Please don't make us go all the way, the area we are going toward looks like it is under heavy attack. I'm begging you—I have two little daughters. I don't want to die."

The school is less than half a mile, I decide I can walk, "Okay, pull over."

The driver comes around to open the back door, thanking me nicely for first, not shooting him, and then for not forcing him down the deadly street. I don't want to be responsible for these clowns' deaths anyway. Once they drop me off, the ambulance speeds away. All that separates me from my goal is one straight street. With rockets falling heavily all around, I hug the right side of the car-lined road, a rocket hits a hundred or a hundred and fifty feet behind me. I hit the ground as the explosion sheds a few false seconds of daylight. In this I see cars flying through the smoke and shrapnel hitting the sides of buildings all around. I pull myself up, I must keep walking. Another hundred feet, I hear a faint yell through my still-pressurized ears from the explosion, "Who is there!"

PLO soldiers, about seven, run from one of the buildings to encircle me, fully armed with AK-47s and RBJ rocket launchers.

Scared at first, I am relieved to recognize their allegiance and their accents, they sound just like me. The group leader asks again

"Who are you?"

"Friend!"

This is a kind of well known pass code among the PLO, you are one of them or live among them if you answer this way.

"Where are you from?" The leader asks again.

"I am from Shatila camp."

"You guys are natural born killers."

I can tell he is not from a camp, maybe South Lebanon. "That is what I hear all the time."

"What do you mean that's what you hear all the time? And why are you walking the street this early in the morning between these falling rockets? Are you suicidal?"

I wonder how many times I will have to hear this today.

"Actually I am, believe it or not, I actually almost took my own life about three hours ago."

He shines his flashlight close to my face, then to my arm that had begun to bleed again since I hit the ground after the rocket.

"Were you hit by the last rocket?"

"No, I'm not that lucky. It's from a sniper earlier today."

All the soldiers break out laughing and the leader says, "Looks like he's a bad sniper."

"Not really, he got the best of me."

I do not elaborate, not wanting to explain the situation.

"Man you seem like a very brave man, but I advise you to get off the streets."

"I have to reach that school," I say, pointing my finger towards it.

"You think you will make it there?"

"Believe me, I have cheated death so many times in my life, I think I will."

"You should know how far you can push your good fortune, I wish you luck my friend."

They allow me to pass, retreating back to their domain in the building. My luck lasts and I arrive quickly to the school. The morning is still dark and I wait for the daylight, not wanting to wake anyone prematurely. I sit in the hallway between rooms, eventually laying down, waking up four or five hours later on the warm tile to the noise of children playing.

I am not looking forward to the final step in my mission as I stand, debating whether to climb the stairs and deliver the news to Abud Alsalam's family directly or tell my mother first. Being closer to these people than I, my mother is also wiser, perhaps more tactful in this kind of situation. I decide on the latter, crossing the ground level room to find my mother in a deep sleep on her mattress. Looking down on her, I notice the material on my right sleeve is stiff as if starched, caked dry with blood. I reprimand myself for almost waking her to this frightening sight, I can at least wash this out before disturbing her in more ways than one.

Retracing my steps I stop a woman to ask where I can find water and she leads me to the only running tap in the building. On the way I explain the blood and my desire to rinse my shirt out. To my consternation I see ten or twelve people carrying empty containers already waiting in line for the trickling faucet. I thank the woman, taking my place at the line's rear thinking to myself that this could take an hour or more. Once here, the woman does not leave, saying in a loud voice to the people, “Are you going to let one of our wounded heroes stand at the end of the line?”

She mistakes me for a PLO fighter, assuming my wound is from battle on the front lines. Being short on time I neglect to correct her, taking the privilege she offered as I pass the people who have moved to the side.

I strip down to my waist, rinsing my sleeve three or four times until it is at least presentable. The duct tape on my arm is black with the dry blood. I unwind it, painfully removing the cotton from around the opening. The bullet wound has left a deep hole, I see my bone as I rinse my whole arm under the water. The people standing by watch silently, I behave as normally as possible.

A woman near the front who has a clear view of my arm exclaims, “Poor guy, the wound might get infected. You might lose your arm.”

She tells me to wait, leaving her place to return soon with white material and a typical red head scarf worn often by Muslim women. She fixes me up, gently tying the scarf to secure the bandage. I thank everyone as I put my shirt back on, reverently they chorus together, “God bless you for your bravery!”

I half-smile while leaving to find my mother once again, she sleeps still. I carefully seat myself on the mattress, my weight on the springs causes her to open her eyes to the sight of me directly in front of her. Her face instantly breaks into a wide smile, she hugs and kisses both my cheeks, telling me I was just in her dreams. After her greeting she asks about the dampness of my sleeve.

“I was washing my hand, the water splashed on my arm.” I

reply, trying to bypass the whole truth to save her the sadness and worries, the news I bring is sad enough.

There is no way to mitigate what I must tell her next, she counts Abud Alsalam as one of her own sons.

"Mom, Abud Alsalam was killed last night."

Both hands cover her open mouth, her face transforms from joy to horror, muffling her moans as she rocks back and forth so as not to wake those sleeping around us. I hold her tightly, shedding a few tears of my own. She pauses between sobs, asking how he died.

"By a sniper."

My mother, a devoutly religious woman, blesses him, "May God have mercy on his soul, forgive his sins if there are any."

Focusing her attention on my next words by turning her face to mine with both my hands, I tell her, "Mom I want you to inform his parents of his death. I do not feel I am the right person for the job."

Head shaking without hesitation, my mother refuses, "No, no. I cannot go upstairs to break both his parents' hearts. Please spare me this torture."

I see she is not willing to finish my mission and I will not force her.

"It's okay mom, I will do it."

In her ensuing silence I sense from her eyes she does not want me to do it either. Kissing her forehead as I leave, I brace myself for what is next as I tell her, "I love you mom."

I return to the hallway and climb the stairs looking in each room of this level for Abud Alsalam's family. Ironically, I never visited his family here while he was alive. In the middle of the hall

I find the room, spotting his father and several older men sitting on short stools and drinking hot tea or coffee. I stand frozen in the doorway hoping he will see me. After a few minutes he does, rising and walking cup still in hand, directly towards me.

"How are you son?" he hails using his familiar name for me, asking, "Why do you not come in?"

I am unable to answer, barely able to keep from crying. His expression changes as he puts his head out of the door looking both ways, "Where is my son? You two are always together."

I cannot stop now from crying, I see he is struck, already knowing in his heart what I have come for.

He screams, "No, no! Not my son!"

His wife hearing her husband's screams runs to where we are at the door. Without having to ask she knows what has happened, falling to the floor slapping her face with both hands. The most terrible sound I have heard comes from this broken-hearted screaming mother. She calls my friend's name as she cries in agony on the ground, increasing my own pain.

My tears come in earnest now, I feel again what I will face now that he is gone.

People gather around us, the women pull his mother aside, sharing her grief with empathetic tears, wailing. The men likewise gather around his father and I try to calm his violent reaction.

The father breaks away from these men, coming to hug me; his embrace is so tight I feel the blood coming again from my wounded arm. Suddenly he stops, wiping his nose and eyes on his pajama sleeve, stopping his tears to ask, "Were you with him when he died?"

"Yes."

He feels my pain, "That must have been hard on you, to see your friend, my son, dying. I don't know how he died, but I know if there was anything you could have done to save my son you would have, you would have taken the bullet for him; I know this without asking. I want you to take me to him."

I nod my head in agreement. Two men in the room, one with a vehicle offers to drive us to him. The father whispers in his wife's ear before leaving with us and she insists on going, "I want to go see my son!"

Her husband soothes her, "Later, let me go find him first."

We all run down the stairs, his father leading the way, not wanting to wait another moment. He takes the front seat beside the driver and the other man and I ride in the back. Once at Shatila, I instruct the driver through the roads. Coming near the narrow street I ask the man to park, knowing his truck will not fit where we must go.

I walk ahead the others following, to find Abud Alsalam. When we round the corner his father stands five feet away, staring at his son. Something happens now that I can hardly believe, something I will never forget as long as I live. All the black hair on his father's head turns gray as the three of us watch. In under a minute this man, who this morning drank coffee with jet black hair now has a fully gray head. I have no explanation for this phenomena, still looking at the man my mind accepts that it has no answer for this.

Without mentioning anything of this to the father we all lean down to carry Abud Alsalam's body to the back of the truck. We drive to the family's house, laying Abud Alsalam in his own bed.

His father asks us to leave him alone with his son and we file out, closing the door behind us. I do not want to leave but the look in his father's eyes leaves me no choice. I thank the men for their help and decide to slip away to the nearby shelter.

From one of the main streets I hear men screaming as I walk; from curiosity I change my path to see what is wrong. I hear the loud sound of a shotgun, soon I am close enough to see the scene: four PLO soldiers beat a skinny man wearing civilian clothes; white shirt, black pants, with a neatly trimmed black beard. I know one of the soldiers. For some reason I involve myself in the situation by asking the soldier that I know what the reason for the beating is.

"He is a spy to the Israelis, we caught him red-handed talking on a radio to them, guiding their rockets to exact locations."

One of the soldiers carries the radio they caught him with. This man is in deep shit. The beating stops temporarily, just long enough for the man to confess to the deceitful crime they charge him with, he yells in our own dialect, "I am very sorry!"

One of the soldiers interjects, "You're not sorry. You're sorry you got caught."

Another soldier pulls his handgun out, dedicating the man's inevitable demise with, "In the name of the Revolution, I put you to death." He shoots the man in the head point blank. The others take turns spitting on his body. Before leaving they strip the traitor naked, an example to all those who would think of betrayal.

Watching all this I think, *What kind of life is this, the Israelis have almost destroyed Beirut, decimated the camps; do they really need help from one of our own?*

Anger builds in me to know that this bastard has been helping the Israelis all along. For some reason I blame the death of Abud Alsalam on him. I take my six click knife and slit his throat. Even though he does not feel this in death, it makes *me* feel better anyway.

The soldiers watch me slice the man, the soldier I know asking, “Do you feel better now?”

“Well, a little, but if you ever catch another one of those alive, would you give me the honor of killing him? Not with a gun, but with this very same knife.”

“You should have asked, I would have given you the honor three minutes ago.”

He assures me the next one they catch will be mine. Still unsatisfied and in a growing rage, I about-face, deciding to return to Abud Alsalam’s house to comfort his father instead of going to see Rola.

The door is open halfway when I reach his house and I am about to knock when the sound of his father crying stops me. I walk around the outside of the house to the window I know is busted in the living room. I raise my head slowly, not wanting to disturb the father-son moment.

The father sits on the brown couch next to his son’s body, he holds a big black leather book, an album. For some reason I cannot understand, he is showing his lifeless son the family pictures, explaining about the times when he was little.

My heart breaks. Anyone would find this strange, maybe crazy even but to me this is normal. Knowing my friend’s father, his big heart explains everything. I back away without a sound, leaving them in the moment undisturbed.

I revert back to my original plan, turning again towards the shelter. Making it back, I see Rola walking around, radio to her ear. I follow discreetly behind her, she smiles when she sees me, lowering the radio as she does.

She seems disturbed when she asks, “Have you heard the news?”

“Is there ever anything good in the news?”

“The Americans or the United Nations are working a deal between the Israelis and the PLO. The deal is that the PLO have to leave Beirut for some other Arabic country.”

Trying to explain her concern, she continues, “This means that all the men in the camps ages twenty to forty-five have to leave; all our friends, families, neighbors.”

I can understand her concern, trying to abate her fears, saying, “I can’t see that happening. If I were you I wouldn’t be that worried.”

She mentions that both parties have agreed on a cease-fire until the negotiations are over.

“Are you sure there will be a cease-fire?”

“Yes! Both sides have promised not to shoot at each other until the talks go through or fail.”

“Well, seems like at least something good is resulting from the negotiations. Now we can breathe a little.”

Knowing Rola has been underground too long, I ask her if she wants to go out practice shooting. There is nowhere to go in the camp. This is the best excuse I can come up with to get her away. She tells me, “I don’t know how to use a gun.”

“It’s okay, I’m going to teach you.”

She is very excited, asking me to wait while she asks her mother for permission. I escort her to the end of the room where we find her mother and another woman talking about the same issue, the PLO leaving Beirut. Rola interrupts the discussion to ask if she can go target shooting with me.

Her mother says, “Not alone, only if I come along.”

I had expected this, right away I jump in with, “That would be an honor. Alright, give me five minutes before you meet me outside the shelter.”

I run to my house choosing one of the five AK-47s there, grabbing a case of ammo, I load the weapon. I take along five extra clips for my handgun as well. When I return I find them already waiting outside and the three of us walk the main street toward Sports City, an old soccer stadium. The way is uphill and the going is steep. Sports City is on the highest hill overlooking the whole of Shatila camp. It takes a while to reach the top and her mother is not as young as we are. She is out of breath when we finally make it, sitting to rest on one of the many old wooden benches in the stadium saying, “You two don’t mind me, go ahead and I’ll wait here.”

She is trying not to be in the way. Rola and I walk to the center of the large sandy space. I lean three empty glass bottles on one of the six-foot walls and retreat about sixty-feet for our lesson. I decide to shoot with the smaller of the two guns, placing my nine millimeter in Rola’s hands as I help position her from behind. I hold her right hand, trying to give her some confidence. I explain how to squeeze the trigger, I am surprised that she starts shooting; finishing the whole clip quickly and laughing the whole time at her poor aim.

I reload, returning to my close position behind her, although this time I do not hold her hand—I just want to be behind her. She starts shooting again with no luck, the targets remain untouched. I see her mother laughing at Rola in the distance. After loading this time I explain how to aim, showing my proficiency by picking off a bottle in one shot. Putting the gun in her hand for the third time; no luck again. I decide it is time for the bigger gun, the semi-automatic AK-47. I want to give her some satisfaction in hitting the remaining targets. I do not think she will miss, the clip of this gun holds thirty bullets. I put the AK-47 in her hands, she sprays the whole area, eventually hitting both bottles. This makes her scream in happiness, proud she has broken the targets successfully at last.

Watching her have so much fun inspires the same feelings in me, for the next hour Rola puts me to work collecting any new targets I can find for her shooting pleasure. Meanwhile her mother walks to us, some of her daughter's happiness reflected on her face as she thanks me for giving her only daughter some fun. I can tell it does her good to see her daughter this way. After Rola spends all my ammo we head back to the shelter. Her mother comments on the walk, "I cannot wait until both of you give me some grand kids."

Rola and I laugh, holding hands all the way to the shelter; this is our dream too.

Outside the shelter door Rola whispers something in my ear that makes my face crimson, her mother watching. She tells me how badly she wants to kiss me. I can only smile.

I don't go back down to the shelter with them, telling Rola, "I will be back later."

I walk next door to the PLO office, trying to find out what is going on; to see if the story I hear from Rola is true. I see soldiers loitering outside talking about the same thing, this is an unusual sight in the daylight. There is an argument between them. Some soldiers say they will not go anywhere. Others say they will follow whatever decision is made. One asks my opinion, "Would you leave, if the decision was made?"

"I am the wrong person to ask, I don't belong to any organization or group in the PLO. I'm not going anywhere."

The same man tells me, "You are a smart guy."

While I listen to the arguing, another soldier joins the group saying, "Well I'm going to Abud Alsalam's burial, aren't you his best friend?"

I am shocked that I have not been informed of the plans. He continues, "They are at the cemetery right now burying him as we speak."

I sprint as fast as I can, the cemetery is on the opposite side of the camp. I will not miss this for anything in the world. I promised Abud Alsalam I would see him decently buried. While running I realize all the time I wasted at Sports City being gone too long to be informed of the burial.

The whole family is at the cemetery in front of Abud Alsalam's body, now wrapped in a white bed sheet spotted with his blood.

Walking straight to give his mother a hug and a kiss on her forehead, I tell her Abud Alsalam's last words: "'Tell my mom to be strong.' "This is the last thing he said before closing his eyes forever."

She stops crying, "If he asked you to tell me that, then his wish is granted. I shall not cry again."

Looking at the body lying next to the freshly dug hole, I kneel to say goodbye to the only person who has stood by me since childhood. I untie the bed sheet just enough to see his face once more, he wears a slight smile I did not notice before. As sad as I am, the smile gives me some peace in my heart. Ruffling his hair with my hand a few times, I finally say, "I am sorry my friend, that the sniper chose you over me."

It seems that his father heard my last words, he kneels next to me saying, "Don't ever question God's will son, only God decides who goes and who stays. Don't forget that."

"Sure," I say, even though I scream to myself that God has nothing to do with this. I let this go, knowing the brokenness of his father's heart.

Some of the family members read passages of the Qur'an as all stand praying. His body is lowered to its final resting place, our bare hands fill the hole with dirt. At the conclusion of the two hour ceremony, this hardest part of the ordeal behind us, we all walk back to the camp.

During this time span a lot has happened in the camp. We return to see many angry people in the streets. They have just heard on the news that Yasser Arafat, the PLO leader, has agreed to evacuate his organization from Beirut to relocate in different Arabic countries like Tunisia and Yemen. The people are outraged, many are saying that accepting these conditions is a shame to all Palestinians. It looks like the agreement has been reached through the U.S. envoy Philip Habib. I hear the PLO have to pull out in exchange for the cease fire. The Israeli army are prohibited from entering Beirut, they must pull out to the original lines set before the invasion.

For the next few days we begin to feel peace with no rockets falling and no snipers shooting. The sadness in the streets still persists. We see the PLO army trucks leaving filled with soldiers armed only with personal weapons, which is acceptable in the agreement with the Israelis. The heavy weaponry is passed on to the new protectors of the city, the armed Lebanese Guerillas. The PLO soldiers gather by the thousands in Elmalab-Elbalady, the National Field, an open playground. There are hundreds of big trucks loaded with PLO soldiers, all congregating in preparation to be shipped out of the region by sea to the different Arabic countries. I watch the whole thing and seeing the familiar faces in the field gives me goose bumps. There are many tears as each soldier leaves his whole family behind. I feel the injustice of the situation, what is happening is not right.

A woman screams, "We are going to be defenseless now!"

All the guys I have grown up with are dead or leaving now for good. I do not stay long, not being able to take the oppressive sadness. I decide to visit Rola, this time at her house. The shelter no longer exists. There is no need for it.

I go straight there and I find her mother outside washing clothes in a large plastic tub. Not thinking before I speak, I say, "Hey mom."

She stops her work, standing to ask me, "Say that again."

After repeating myself, she comes close to tell me, "Please, from now on call me that."

I ask where Rola is and her mom points me to the kitchen where she is cooking as usual.

"Smells good, what are you cooking?"

"Beans and cow meat. Cow meat, not dogs, not human."

By this time each household has plenty of meat, part of the agreement specified that food be allowed inside the city, especially to the camps. Cow meat has flooded in from many European countries, free food from every direction. She says something nice now, "This time I am cooking for you my love. Can I ask you something to do for me?"

"Yes, anything."

"I want you to take me to say goodbye to the soldiers."

She wants me to take her to the place I have just left. Even though I hate the idea not wanting to go back, I recognize this is the first time she has asked me to do something just for her.

"Okay, I'll take you."

"Okay let's go."

"Now?"

"Yes, my mom will take over the cooking."

I have no choice. Having already assented to the idea, I am obligated. We walk outside, informing her mother of where we are going and she grants us her blessing. We walk fifteen minutes to that damned place, to the field of soldiers but the walk is lovely. Rola is full of life, jumping happily around me, happy to be together without fear. I hold her right hand, forcing her to calm down a little.

Nearing the field, we hear a lot of shooting, sounds like AK-47s. Soldiers shooting up in the air, for celebration? I do not know. Thousands of families are saying their farewells, everyone is saying goodbye to everyone. Kisses abound between soldiers and families, I have never seen so many tears in one place. Having

been here a matter of minutes, I look over to see Rola already bawling. This makes me smile in spite of the sober atmosphere. The contrast between her behavior on the walk and now makes me wonder at the range of human emotions.

A high ranking PLO officer climbs a low-rise stage. The people gather around to listen to his motivational speech. He shouts that we are not retreating, not leaving Beirut with our heads in the mud. We have never raised the white flag. We never will. Yasser Arafat has agreed to this evacuation for one reason, to protect the innocent civilians especially in the refugee camps.

An older woman interrupts the speech with screams, "How does he expect to protect the civilians and the people in the camps when the PLO soldiers are leaving us? I thought this revolution was created to fight Israel to the last soldier, to take back our land, Palestine. How will we be protected? Who is going to protect the women, children and elderly men?"

The PLO officer replies, "Mr. Arafat made an agreement. This is one of the main deals that he made that will prevent the Israeli army from ever entering the city again. Therefore Beirut and the refugee camps in Beirut are going to be protected."

An elderly man, in his mid-seventies screams, "America! You made an agreement with America and Israel! They gave you their word they would not enter Beirut!? Isn't America our enemy number one, Israel enemy number two, and you guys trust both of these enemies with our lives?"

The high ranking official hesitated to answer, the interruptions have turned the crowd against his optimism. More begin to scream in agreement, shouting, "This agreement shows the PLO and Yasser Arafat as cowards!"

The same old man continues, "Not only the Israelis and the United States but we are surrounded by other enemies as well. The Christian Lebanese, we have been feuding with for years in the civil war. You are taking away our young men, the ones who are supposed to be defending us? This is bullshit!"

By now the PLO official realizes he cannot continue. He steps away with his retinue of armed body guards who whisk him away from the angry crowd. The old man screams after the retreating official, "May God have mercy on the people in the camps! No one else will have mercy on us!"

I feel the old man's experience forecasts the end of this conflict better than my experience can. His reasoning makes sense.

We stay maybe two or three hours watching batches of men come say farewell, cry, then leave. It looks like this has been going on all day. I get the opportunity to send off a few of my family members, cousins, and other personal friends.

I feel we have stayed long enough, and ask Rola, "Are you ready to go home?"

She pleads with swollen eyes, "Can we stay one more hour?"

"How much more crying do you want?"

"I'm not crying!"

"No, you cried enough, let's go."

She concedes, "Okay," knowing she has no choice.

I feel I have to pull her away from that place. We walk back hand-in-hand, talking the whole way. She is still stronger than I, having no problem expressing her feelings for me openly. I know I have to save my long-awaited profession of those three words for exactly the right moment.

We arrive at her house and once inside she takes authority of dinner right away, setting the table and after sitting me down says, "Sit here and don't do anything. I am going to serve you."

It is nice sitting around a dinner table, it has been too long; close to three months since the war began. The food is so delicious, I eat until I can barely breathe. After dinner her mother asks about my mother and I tell her, "Well, my mom is still scared to return home. She is going to stay a little bit longer at the school until she feels it is safe to return."

Rola's mother replies, "It seems safe now. There is not much water, but there is a lot of food."

There is only one operating water tap in the whole camp. "That reminds me," she says, "there isn't much water at home, I need to go get some."

Feeling I am the man of the house now, I offer my services, "No, I'll go get you some water."

She hands me two empty gallon jugs and I carry these to the tap where many people already wait in the line. I wait with them and the whole errand takes over an hour. I return with the filled gallons putting them inside the door. I inform Rola, "I have to go."

She asks me to stay, to spend the night. I feel this is not appropriate, to stay in a house alone with two women. To her mother I am still somewhat a stranger, it is better if I go. Her mother overhears the conversation and she too comes close to offer a personal invitation for me to stay. She would feel safer if I did. I can accept these terms and agree to stay. With this Rola runs to her bedroom, excitedly grabbing bedding for me. I will sleep on the roof.

Once I settle into my sentry position on the roof, Rola comes to my side as I look down on the streets. There are hardly any bodies left, the smell of them is disappearing in the beautiful late August evening. Rola comments, "It is nice to finally have peace, no loud explosions, no gunshots."

In this peace Rola and I talk about our future, where we will live after we marry, our feelings for each other. Of course I tell her how beautiful her brown eyes are in the full moonlight. My eyes cannot move from her face, the most lovely sight they can behold.

We talk about everything imaginable, even down to what we will name our children. Being on the roof with her like this in the enchanted evening reminds me I am the luckiest man alive. We agree that the day of our marriage is very near, everything peaceful and right. This idea is very exciting, being and living together until death do us part. I feel the roof is full of love. Still something holds back the three words even in the perfect moment. I am closer than ever, whatever has held me back fades slowly away.

The time is close to four in the morning, Rola's eyes are sleepy and I ask her to go get some rest but as usual she wants to stay just a little bit longer. I assure her that from now on there is no other place I will be. She will see me tomorrow and every day after that. This gives her the confidence to say good night and go downstairs to sleep next to her mother. I lay down on the mattress, counting the fading stars in the morning sky. One thought is on my mind: how lucky and blessed I am to have survived this war; not only me, but also the girl I love more than anything in the universe. These thoughts lead me to remember Abud Alsalam, how he died only one day before this peace.

I had come perilously close to taking my own life, the thought of missing the bliss of tonight chills me even as I mourn my best friend. Only now I feel that my survival is for a reason, whatever reason, I hope it will be revealed to me in the coming future. I fall asleep to these hopeful thoughts.

I wake later in the morning around eleven, refreshed from my deep sleep. I run downstairs, searching for my girl Rola. She is folding clean clothes in the living room but on seeing me she drops everything to run jumping into my arms as if she has not seen me in ages. Slightly embarrassed and not wanting her mother to see the scene, I push her an arm's length away to take in the sight of her. Her hair is clean, shiny black and she wears fresh new clothes. I cannot help but notice the makeup, the first I have ever seen on the already beautiful face; a woman stares into my eyes. Seeing her freshness I become conscious of my own rumpled state, still wearing the same army uniform from the PLO that bandaged my arm. Jealous, I tell her, "I want to go home to take a shower and change into fresh civilian clothes, I want to look good for you too."

She asks why I don't shower at her house. There are plenty of fresh clothes left from her dead brothers. I remind her of my height, six feet at age eighteen. Her brothers were considerably shorter than I. I would have consented except I feel the need to check on and redress my arm, I have kept this from Rola. I promise her, "I will go clean up and return to take you to the National Field to watch the last batch of PLOs leaving Lebanon."

This makes her happy. I know she enjoys the drama. Hearing the bargain she agrees. I walk to my house this time not tripping on or even seeing any rotting bodies. The PLO had cleaned out the streets before they left. The pleasant walk takes only five minutes. Once at home I pick up the water pails, needing water to clean up. I find only three people waiting in line for the tap, almost everyone is at the National Field to see the last of the soldiers off.

With the containers filled in no time, I return to bathe, aided by a plastic cup and a bar of soap manufactured from pure olive oil. This kind of soap is popular and easily acquired in the camps. Scooping the cups of water over my head feels heavenly, this is my first shower in more than two and a half months. I feel the filth and dirt running off me as I scrub with a loofa, the rinse water turns brown. The feel of the water seems to wash away all the sadness and suffering of the war. I feel great and my whole body weight is lighter after ridding myself of the dirt. I don civilian clothes from my drawer, a black shirt with blue jeans. Wearing a color different than green is strange, the feel of them is foreign on my body. I comb my hair, looking in the mirror to see a different person. I am in fine form now to see Rola, I am eager to find her as I rush out the door down the street to her house.

August 31, 1982

The Last day of the PLO evacuation from Beirut.

I find Rola sitting on the steps outside waiting for me and the first thing she calls out is, "I am ready, I am so excited!"

"We are not going to a movie theatre. We're going to a depressing place."

She snaps back, "You don't understand, what we will be

watching is history. We should be there so we can remember and tell our kids."

I laugh, "Okay genius, let's go."

She passes me a package wrapped in newspaper, saying, "Here's something for you."

I find inside a pita bread sandwich filled with fried meat, chopped fresh onions and tomatoes. Ecstatically grateful, I eat it on the way as once again Rola jumps around me like a child. Her excitement forces smiles to my face between bites.

"What has gotten into you?"

Wearing a huge smile she replies, "Nothing! I'm just so excited and happy to see you, that's all."

"Okay, now you are happy but just wait until you get there."

Unfazed, she shoots back, "Yeah, until we get there I am going to be happy!"

Passing the doorway to the National Field, I already sense her face falling to one of sadness. Thousands of people from all over Beirut have come to say goodbye to the last group of PLO. I see nothing but tearful farewells. Bullets fire constantly from soldiers who shoot in the air from the trucks that take them away from their homes and families forever.

I hear one question countless times from women, especially older women, "Who is going to protect us now? We are going to be defenseless without you guys!"

Each time Rola overhears this she cries even harder. We spend almost the whole day here, not fun at all, staying until the last soldier is loaded on the last truck, heading for the port.

Wrapping my arm around her shoulders, I say, "Okay, let's go back to the camp, there is nothing else to do here."

On the way Rola's sadness has carried over, depressed as could be. She repeats the question we have heard all day, "Who is going to defend us if the Israelis decide to attack the camps?"

"I don't think that is possible, the Israelis and the PLO signed an agreement with the Americans through their envoy Philip Habib that they will not enter Beirut after the PLO evacuation. How can they attack if they never enter Beirut?"

She asks a question now that I have no answer to, "Do you trust the Americans and the Israelis?"

I stop her, pausing for a minute before answering, "Well, Yasser Arafat seems to trust them. We trust Yasser Arafat's judgment, don't we?"

I know this man is Rola's role model, Yasser Arafat is loved by all the younger generation in the camps.

"Yes I trust Yasser Arafat, even though I'm scared."

"Don't be, I am here to protect you because you're my girl."

I think that this last thing is what will make her feel good, not the political promises. Her arms wrap around my waist, her head rests on my chest, a moment passes before she tells me, "I know you are going to be there for me. You will be there to protect me. This alone makes me feel safe. I trust nobody but you."

Tightly returning her embrace, I lift her head to kiss her forehead. She lifts her eyes, saying, "I love you so much, you were there for me and my mom, for everyone in the shelter. You stood as one man taking care of all of us. I know you can take care of two women, me and my mom."

When she finishes I return the affection with, "You make me feel the same. I am so happy around you; for this I am thankful, to you and your mom."

I see tears ready to fall from her eyes, changing the subject to spare her any more tears, interrupting with, "Let's get going before your mom gets worried."

We walk quietly the rest of the way, finding her mother fixing dinner at their house. Right away Rola's mom asks how the day was, referring to the last PLO evacuation. She wants to hear everything, every boring detail. Rola begins describing the scene and her mother cries, starting Rola up again. Two women crying in the kitchen. I stand aloof, listening to Rola and I think to myself that her mother must have a great amount of trust in me by allowing her cherished daughter to spend the day in my care. I feel privileged to hold this position of trust. Rola is her sole remaining child, the last hope of an entire family.

* * * * *

From this moment life is sweet. Water and food rush into the camp. The idea of peace becomes familiar, tangible. I get the feeling we will all be just fine. Life is much different from the peace before the war. Virtually all young men from the camps are absent, I see only the elderly, women and children.

I begin to think Yasser Arafat has in fact done the right thing. I have never known peace. All my life has been war, first the civil war then this Israeli invasion.

The thought dawns slowly in my mind that there may be more to life than war and violence. Spending every moment possible with Rola, I discover a lifestyle of love, a reality in happiness.

Day after day Rola and I grow closer, my love for her flourishes. We come to know each other well, I know deep in my soul I cannot live one day without her.

I decide it is time to make formal arrangements, making the journey to the refugee school to see my mother. She is still unready to return to her house, not feeling the same peace I am experiencing. In the large room sitting next to my mother, I face her seriously and begin to explain,

"While I have been in the camp during the war Rola and I have gotten to know each other well. We have fallen deeply in love."

My mother interrupts to say, "What you are saying makes me very happy, Rola is not only very, very beautiful but she has a huge heart too. I got to know her during my stay in the shelter, she cared for me and everyone there—a true hero. She even entertained the children to distract them from being afraid as the rockets fell."

I find my mother explaining to me my own feelings about Rola, I am relieved at her appreciation for my prospective bride.

She is already ahead of me, saying, "You are here to ask my permission to marry her."

I smile, "You have always been smarter than anyone I know mom."

Right away she answers her own question, "You have my blessing, I wish both of you happiness!" She hugs me as she sheds tears, this time of happiness. Now having the blessing of both our mothers, Rola and I have no hindrances in planning the wedding for the first of the coming new year. I do not want to rush the date. There is still too much sadness in the camp; grieving women still wear black, each family mourning the two or three members lost in the recent war. A wedding in this setting would be improper.

Things are improving, little grocery stores opening again, cars driving through the streets, the prospect of normal life grows with each passing day.

September 11, 1982

I listen to the radio in the living room of my house as I clean, readying the place for my mother's scheduled return in a week. I stop when a serious announcement breaks in on the radio program….

"This is a special announcement. The Israeli Defense Minister, Ariel Sharon, has announced that two-hundred PLO soldiers have remained inside the Palestinian refugee camps."

I think this news is strange; living in the camp, I know for certain that if any soldiers remain I would have known. I blow the announcement off, continuing my chore. Half an hour later the same news is repeated, I begin to worry. Whatever reason is behind this announcement is not good.

Going out to the street, I see people grouped together discussing this development, everyone wonders what will come of this worrisome political move. The older women all agree that this is a bad omen. That something bad is about to happen to those of us who remain in the Palestinian refugee camps.

The next three days are tense, the only talk is of what will happen.

Shortly after this, some group or individual assassinates the Lebanese President-elect, Bashir Gemayal. This is the worst thing that could happen to the Lebanese people, who are looking forward to a peaceful country.

The assassination adds more fuel to the worried conversations around camp. Everyone is asking, "Who would murder the Lebanese President-elect? He has not even taken office yet, and already he has been killed?"

We do not wait long for the answer to all our questions. The very next day five or six hundred Israeli tanks move into West Beirut, moving from there to totally occupy the city. They have one purpose: to surround the Palestinian refugee camps.

The tanks roll straight to the camps, completely encircling and sealing both Sabra and Shatila from the rest of the world.

CHAPTER FOUR

Preparation for a Massacre

By mid-day on the 15th of September, 1982, the refugee camps are entirely surrounded by Israeli tanks and soldiers. Checkpoints are installed at strategic locations and crossroads around the camps, enabling the invasion force to monitor all the entries and exits. No one is allowed to leave. The people are scared, wondering what is going on; we all agree on one point, that all of this has something to do with Ariel Sharon's claim that two hundred PLO soldiers remain hidden among us. Both Sabra and Shatila are under full Israeli occupation. The people inside ask each other in bewilderment what has happened to the signed diplomatic agreement between Yasser Arafat on one side, and the Americans and Israelis on the other. They repeat over again in disbelief the situation they have found themselves in. The reason the PLOs agreed to leave was so that the Israeli army would not enter Beirut.

I am with Rola outside her house as we watch tanks roll down the main street. She is horrified just looking at the tanks that have come to destroy the short peace of the camp rolling right outside her door. She asks me, "Are they going to kill us?"

I try my best to calm her down, saying, "They can't just kill us. Remember, the Americans promised Arafat that no one in the camps will be harmed."

"The Americans also promised the Israelis would not enter Beirut! What makes you think they will not break the second promise and not kill us all?!"

I see I am not making any progress in calming Rola's fears. We watch the Israeli soldiers treat the elderly men and women in the street disrespectfully, pushing them around and spitting on them. I am scared too, I feel the Israeli army is up to something horrible.

Speakers mounted on large trucks announce to the people of the camp that now is the time to surrender any weapons they may have. Promising they will not be harmed in the process. The speakers also say that we have two hours to comply, any weapon found in the camp after this time will bring a severe punishment for the entire family. No one wants to risk communal punishment so all hurriedly gather weapons to throw on the growing pile in front of the Israelis on the main street. I stand watching the show, debating whether to give up my nine millimeter handgun or not. Not wanting to take a chance with Rola and her mother's safety, I

retrieve the gun from beneath my mattress on the roof. Under the suspicious looks of the Israeli soldiers, I throw it onto the pile with the others. When the two hour deadline passes, a large army truck is loaded with the pile of weapons and drives away with our last line of defense.

The Israeli army now knows for a fact that both camps are clean of any weapons. They know no one will take a chance on their threat of punishment. I am sure Sharon now knows his theory on the remaining two hundred PLOs is false, if he is in communication with his soldiers. A former military man himself, communication is certain.

The army has taken Sports City as its main base, where once I had taken Rola target shooting. From this high ground they overlook all of Shatila camp, able to see any and all movement. Sports City is less than a quarter mile from the camp's center and both camps find themselves completely under the Israeli military's mercy. I watch the Israeli soldiers behave as if we are the prizes of their victory, as if they can treat us however they please. One realization hits me; there is nothing worse than to be occupied by your own enemy.

One or two hours later these soldiers pull out of the camps to their new base at Sports City. It seems Shatila, for their own amusement, has become a personal target for the soldiers' practice, bullets showering the camp from the direction of the hill. This continues for hours, the people huddling in houses for fear of becoming a casualty of their fun. A call goes out by word of mouth for all men to meet in an old PLO office to attempt a solution to end the target practice.

In the meeting full of elderly men discussing what to do, there is an agreement. Five of the high profile elder men, all between the ages sixty-five and seventy-five, are to be sent to meet with the Israeli officer in charge and talk of stopping the needless shooting on the camp.

These five men are wished luck before they ascend the hill to Sports City. The rest of us sit tight in the office, anxiously awaiting the men's return. Three, four, five hours pass; the men haven't returned. I tire of waiting and decide to go check on Rola and her mom. I find them still frightened and sitting in the middle of the living room, holding each other. They both run to me as I enter, apparently waiting for my safe return.

They ask about the nature of the meeting that was called for the men and I fill them in on the general happenings, ending by explaining my impatience when the five men did not return. Rola's mother screams hysterically, "Why don't those Israelis go back where they came from! They are going to kill us all, I can feel it!"

"That is impossible, the world is watching," I attempt to reason.

She is not listening. "The world does not care about us! Nobody cares about us!" she continues to scream.

It seems to me she has convinced herself that the Israelis plan to have their revenge. Suddenly her anger switches to Yasser Arafat. "How could Arafat just leave us defenseless like this. He doesn't care about us, he cares only about himself!" she cries in anger.

Still trying to calm her, I tell her, "I'm sure they discussed all this in their negotiations before the agreement was reached with the Americans and Israelis."

"You have seen with your own eyes the way they are treating us. Weren't you outside watching? Didn't you see the tanks in the streets looking ready for war?"

By this time it has grown dark and I think of leaving for my own home but cannot stomach the thought of leaving these women in their terror. Without needing or asking permission, I decide to stay the night with them. Rola's mother is tired and I ask them to go to bed together, feeling Rola should be near to keep her mother company. I assure them both I am not going anywhere, telling them I will wake them if anything happens.

Once they are in bed I walk the stairs to the roof, from there I see tanks still moving, all climbing the hill to reinforce the base at Sports City. Five or six foot soldiers accompany each tank, the loud engines continue until almost five in the morning. By this time I am exhausted, laying my head on the mattress left from my last stay. I slip unknowingly to sleep.

I wake to a sweet kiss on my left cheek. I open my eyes to the most beautiful face just inches from my own.

"Good morning my love," is the sweet sound that accompanies the sweet kiss.

I reply with a big smile, "Good morning beautiful."

"We are still alive," she says.

"What did you think was going to happen? Of course we are still alive," I answer.

"I know you are hungry, I'm going downstairs to fix you some breakfast."

I rise to follow her down, watching her every move while she prepares my meal. Fried eggs and cheese, hot tea; my pleasure is not in the food, it is in beholding Rola's joy in her movements in the kitchen. So unlike the night before, the morning has renewed the strength I have always so admired in her. Just she and I share the table, enjoying the private breakfast while her mother still sleeps. Finishing breakfast, I smile shyly saying, "I'm going to have to get used to this."

She moves near, "If this makes you happy, I will love to fix you breakfast, lunch and dinner for the rest of my life."

Of course this is music to my ears, giving some peace to my heart even in the uncertainty of what will happen with the invasion. How, where, or when I have no idea, but I cannot shake the feeling that something bad is poised to overtake the people here. I hope I am wrong.

I stand, telling Rola I need to check on my parent's house to make sure the Israelis have not broken in. I still anticipate the return of my mother, plus I wonder at the fate of the five men who went up the hill. Rola jumps to stand in front of the door, telling me, "Don't worry about me and my mom, we will be fine. Go take care of the things you need to do."

I am happy to see her optimistic attitude, as I begin to step out she catches my right hand, pulling me back. "I want you to know I love you, that I will love you as long as I live."

I lean down to kiss her right cheek, "I will see you soon," are my farewell words as I head to the old PLO office I left the night before. I find only four men remaining, I ask if there is any news.

"No, they have not returned," is the sober reply I get.

My suspicions are that the five messengers may be dead. I think as I walk away that I am glad my mother has not returned

from the refugee school yet. I hope she will stay a little while longer until I know what will happen here. Again I head home, knowing I must finish the cleaning that I don't want my mother to have to do after her homecoming.

My house is in the middle of the camp. When I get closer I see that the door hanging wide open. I go inside to investigate, searching even under beds; no one is here. I return to finish cleaning the living room and I glance out the window to see movement in Abud Alsalam's house. I can't recognize who it is so I decide to walk over to check. The door here is open as well and I walk in not knowing what to expect. To my relief I find Abud Alsalam's mother cleaning out the dust left from all the rockets. Seeing me, she drops the beating stick she carries to give me a big hug. I can tell she is very happy to see me, perhaps because I remind her of her son.

"How are you doing?" she asks sadly.

"I'm fine, how are you holding up?"

Before she can say anything, tears that fall from her eyes answer for her, "Thank God for everything."

I feel bad for carelessly asking such a question. The last thing I want is to bring this woman more grief. I try again, asking, "How is your husband doing?"

Still crying, she manages, "He is fine, but he has changed a lot since the death of Abud Alsalam."

I understand, losing a son is never easy. I look for an acceptable exit, not wanting to talk any longer and upset the woman any more.

"I'll be next door. If you ever need me just let me know."

I walk back to my house to finish the living room and the rest of the cleaning. It is still early, maybe eight or eight-thirty. Having only two hours of sleep the night before, I collapse on my bed thinking to myself that another couple hours of sleep will help me regain strength. I am shocked out of sleep in the late afternoon or early evening by a screaming woman close by. I stand suddenly in my room, disoriented, having overslept. Overheated and sweating in the small hot space, I down a tall glass of water at my bedside in one drink.

The hysterical woman is coming closer and I run out the door to stop her. I hold her shoulders in both hands, asking, "What is the matter?"

She wails, "They are killing everybody!"

"Where?!" I ask.

"On Dalal El Mograbi Street!"

This is the main street connecting Sabra to Shatila.

CHAPTER FIVE

The Massacre Begins

September 16, 1982. It is Thursday, almost evening and I run towards the street the woman named. As I near, the screams grow louder and I know I cannot travel on the streets any further. Remembering the game Abud Alsalam and I used to play as boys traveling to school, I climb the cement roof of the nearest house, most buildings' metal roofs were replaced in the late seventies. Jumping from rooftop to rooftop is a safer shortcut, the higher ground gives me an advantage. I run and jump at breakneck speed, I am terrified. Rola lives on Dalal El Mograbi Street.

I encounter bedlam below me when I arrive, from the low-rise roof I see people running from their houses to the main street, everyone screaming. I cannot tell what is going on. A woman clutching two little girls, both no more than three or four-years-old, runs my direction from an alley across the way. A man in a green military uniform chases them from behind. He raises an axe, striking the back of the woman's head; she collapses forward onto the little girls.

I look to the left of the street; people everywhere are being chopped down by men wielding axes. Screams surround me from all sides. Not being able to see down that end of the street where Rola's house is, I jump and hang on the ledge of the much higher roof next door on my right. Pulling myself up, I see five or six ropes hung with drying laundry and farther on at the left-most corner of the roof there are several huge carpet rugs rolled loosely standing on end. Reacting without having to think, I walk shielded by the laundry to the rugs. I halfway unroll the outermost rug, standing easily in the tall damp hiding place. My six clicks knife serves to cut a one by six inch rectangular lookout hole facing the street.

The Cinema El Shark, the East Cinema, is at the edge of my vision through the hole to the right. I direct my vision to the left so I can see all the way down that side of the street, where most of the carnage is happening.

Watching from here, I see now that there are hundreds of soldiers, not just the handful I thought when I first climbed the roof. Most of the soldiers wear a red fabric patch on their shoulder but from here I cannot read what is written on them. They carry axes, swords and big knives. It hits me that there is only one reason why these primitive weapons are being used instead of bullets; so as not to alert the houses around and behind—their next targets. The soldiers' objective is to kill the largest number of people possible.

The soldiers run in groups of three or four from house to house. Each time this happens the house erupts in screams temporarily, then within a few moments the screams are cut short. When the screaming stops I can only imagine that the people in the house have been murdered.

One young barefoot woman coming nearer in the street arrests my attention. She is eight or nine months pregnant and the thin white house robe she wears stretches tightly across her overly extended belly. In the sunlight I see her black undergarments, she waddles slowly, holding her stomach as five soldiers goad her on from behind. They seem to enjoy their task, roughly pushing the woman from behind so that she falls to the hard asphalt on her knees every ten to fifteen feet. Each time she falls the soldiers take turns pulling her back up by her hair. Her robe is short, just above her bloody knees; the hem stained red from her spills on the asphalt, lines of blood striping her calves down to her toes.

As she walks the soldiers laugh raucously as they swing their axes and swords right in front of the woman's face. From a distance I see her mouth moving as she cries, I cannot make out in all the screaming what it is she says. I do not understand what the men are after, what they mean to do with this woman. Pushing her on past my building, they stop near an army truck about twenty feet from my right side. Black painted pipes frame over this part of the street a triangular logo picturing an AK-47 on a white background, the symbol for one of the PLO divisions.

The group of soldiers stop the woman here, one running to retrieve from the back bed of the truck two sharp metal s-hooks often used when hanging sides of beef. Passing one to another man, the soldier grabs the woman's shoulder, ramming the hook forcefully through under the clavicle until it protrudes through her back. His partner follows suit with the opposite shoulder as the woman's head shakes violently back and forth; this is the first time I have seen crying and screaming together at this level. By this time I hear the woman's words, over and over. She screams, "You know God is watching right now, he is watching, why are you doing this!"

Blood pumps from the wounds in her shoulders as the men hoist her from under the arms to hook her onto the metal pipe structure, first one hook, then the other. The whole front of her once white gown is bright red and flowing with blood as she still screams. She is hanging about two and a half feet off the ground directly under the PLO insignia and facing me. Of all the horror playing out down the length of the street to my left, this scene has my full attention. The fifth soldier, the one from behind the group, strides forward unsheathing the sword strapped at his side. In one movement he stabs straight into the woman under her rib cage, slicing down as if pulling a lever once, twice, three times until her whole front side down to the birth canal bursts wide open. The clear amniotic fluid-like water rushes from her womb, another soldier thrusts his hand inside the gaping flesh, seizing the inverted unborn baby by the back of its neck. Pulling the baby out of her, the umbilical cord hangs connecting the still-conscious mother and child. Her eyes wide with disbelief, she watches her premature baby in the open air. I think never in her most horrible nightmares could she imagine to have such a delivery.

The soldier holding the baby takes two steps back, ripping the birth cord out of the mother before slamming the child to the

pavement. The infant goes flat on the asphalt. Its mother still watching, the soldier lifts his right foot high directly over her baby, crushing its head like a sweet melon completely to the ground, scraping his foot back to smear the brain with the dirt underfoot. This is the last thing the dying mother sees before screaming, "God!" as her head drops to her chest.

Hearing the mother's last word, I know God is watching; what I do not understand is why God has unleashed devils on these defenseless people; women, children, the elderly. Of course, I find no answer for this question.

I become aware of the smothering heat in the damp carpet, drops of sweat roll from my scalp into my eyes. I am unwilling to bring my hand to wipe away the sting, the slightest movement may shake the roll of carpet close around me; detection at this point is sure to cost me my life.

At this grim conclusion, my eyes turn to meet even more horrifying scenes. Four soldiers drag Mr. Tooki by his hands. He is an older gentleman in his sixties who owns a small grocery store not far across the street from my position. As they drag him, Mr. Tooki's plastic artificial leg detaches, dropping off in the middle of the street. The soldiers find this humorous, pausing to laugh. One soldier retrieves the leg, brings it back to the old man and starts to bludgeon him on the head with the heavy plastic leg twenty to thirty times until he passes away

This man has been a father figure to all the boys in the camp, telling us stories in his shop where we would go to buy or beg for cigarettes. Often he would sell me a pack on credit just for the asking, he would always benevolently answer, "Just pay whenever you can."

Seeing this old harmless man I know so well die mercilessly on the street turns my stomach, he never hurt a fly. Still conscious of my perilous hiding place, I slowly crouch down to vomit, careful not to disturb the carpet around me. Down on my knees, I think of Rola, desperately hoping she has escaped from this massacre. While I hope, my mind races thinking of how to make it to her house without exposing myself to the murderers. It is impossible. I stand to bear witness as my people perish around me, there is nothing else I can do.

In the heat of the small space, trapped by fear, under the intense pressure of not being able to reach Rola and seeing the carnage below me, I snap. A kind of nervous and physical break down seizes me, I can only mouth Rola's name over and over, stomping my foot mechanically as I strain my eyes toward that end of the street as far as possible. My clothes, shoes and socks are saturated with sweat. I begin hallucinating, losing touch with reality as I hope all of this is my mind playing tricks on me. It is a passing nightmare; I close my eyes tightly, thinking I will wake any moment from this gruesome and hideous dream.

Looking down on the butchers in army uniforms, I wonder who these men are, where they are from? Are they human like me?! Their shape is human, but there is nothing human about them. I ask myself, "Is this the judgment day that everybody fears?"

Nothing can be worse than what I witness that day, what I am seeing is contrary to what any religion known to human kind would permit or condone. All moral laws are violated before me, this is worse than the jungle law; the men kill, but not to eat. What then drives these demonized men; money, revenge, or something beyond the scope of my youthful imagination? Are these butchers

Israelis or some other blood thirsty fiends? These thoughts rush through my mind, then I am pulled away by a new sight.

My eyes follow an army Jeep mounted with a ten foot long antennae rolling down the hill from Sports City, the Israeli army's base. The vehicle stops in the middle of the intersection of the main road in front of me, purposely blocking the entrance of the steep road. Four doors fly open and five fully armed soldiers climb out, one wearing the stars of an officer. The five soldiers line up facing the action in front of them. Two in front quickly shield their eyes from the killing, turning their backs after a few seconds with arms overhead to lean on the Jeep, not wanting to watch. The others seem affected differently, standing with drawn weapons watching intently. The soldier at the officer's side has strapped on his back a radio communication box.

I cannot place the men in their role of the massacre, are they posted here to prevent any people from escaping death?

The Jeep and men do not hold my attention. A young naked woman, shaking and dripping blood from her thighs walks unsteadily before two soldiers holding axes. Quickly two more men come towards her, shoving her against a house wall opposite the street, thirty feet in front of the Israeli soldiers near the Jeep. Spreading her feet roughly, their axes are leaned against the wall, the two men now pull their pants down with free hands and begin to take turns raping the woman. The original two soldiers who followed behind her are clapping, enthusiastically cheering their comrades on, their heads thrown back in laughter

I do not wonder any longer at the role of the soldiers standing nearby at the blocked intersection who have declined to stop this gross rape; they are observers as well as hosts of this event. The four soldiers, finished with the bleeding woman, let her go with a sharp kick in the butt. She returns the way she came. I only imagine her life is spared so she can live with the shame of the crime committed against her.

A soldier emerges from a side street one house down on my side of the street with a young boy, no more than two years old, sitting on his shoulders. The man holds the boy's hands high, playing with and swinging the child as any good father would. Once in the middle of the street, he yells towards the four soldiers who just finished their raping, "Shofo, shofo!" (Look, look!) Trying to get their attention.

One of the four screams back, laughing, "You pig! Are you going to rape the little boy?"

The soldiers are speaking Arabic, speaking Arabic in the local Lebanese accent. It hits me—these are not Israelis, they are Lebanese!

"Why are the Lebanese killing us?" I gasp in shock. It must be for revenge, this is the only thing that could turn humans into the devils manifested here.

I know for a fact that all the old women's predictions have come true, the PLO are absent now when they are most needed for protection. These are guerillas, Christian Lebanese who the PLO have fought in the civil war for years, my whole life. The cowards take advantage of the helpless Palestinian people left behind without defense in the camps.

The soldier lowers the boy to the ground, standing him on his feet. Now having the other soldiers' rapt attention, he grabs the

child's ankles just above his small white tennis shoes, carrying him to the same blood stained cement wall that the woman was just raped against. Swinging him back for added momentum, the soldier slams the child head first against the wall again and again. On the third impact I see three quarters of the boy's head fly off, a white substance, his brain, follows. Seven times in all the small body meets the hard surface; the killer, now finished with his fun throws the tiny body to the middle of the street. His audience of four compatriot butchers gather round to pat him on the back for a job well done.

My eyes dart back to the Israelis, aghast that these scenes can continue uninterrupted. One soldier cries, pointing at the boy in the street while saying something I cannot decipher to the soldier next to him; he is losing it. The soldier he speaks with comforts him by pulling the crying man to lean his head on his chest, petting his face while staring at the murdered boy's body strewn in the street.

A group of Lebanese guerillas gather down the street, herding between sixteen and twenty screaming old men, women and children to the center of the road. All of a sudden, without warning, the killers fall upon the people with swords and axes. Within seconds the whole group lies in a heap, blood flowing in dark lines down the pavement to pool in one of the innumerable rocket holes directly in my line of sight.

Now I put the pieces together; there is no intention to spare any lives within the camps; I am certain the whole population is going to be wiped out to the last child and infant.

One lone elderly woman, in her mid-sixties, wanders out obliviously from a side street to behold the freshly slaughtered

pile of people, her shocked reaction indicates that the surrounding streets are unaware of what is happening to their neighbors.

As she jumps and screams in shock, a killer grabs the woman's shoulder by her flowered blue dress. Dragging his victim along he stops fifty or sixty feet from my look-out, demanding of the woman that she remove the many gold bangles she wears on both wrists. Terrified she hunches over, desperately trying to shove the jewelry off between her knees as the man impatiently slaps his thighs and waves his arms, yelling, "Yala, yala!" (Come on, come on!).

She pleads that she can get them off if he gives her time. The killer is out of patience and resumes his dragging, this time pulling the woman from the dress's bodice. Reaching the same truck that the meat hooks were pulled from for the hanging pregnant woman, he removes an axe from the large side cargo pocket of his pants. Pushing the bangles back on the screaming old woman's arms, he forces her right hand on the truck's hood. He chops her hand cleanly off above the wrist, the freed bracelets slide off her wrist to clink on the hood among the spurts of blood that coat the truck's windshield, hood and grill. He repeats the process with her left hand, shoving the hysterical woman away by her chest when finished, her amputated arms arc blood to paint red half-circles on the road as she falls backward.

While the woman writhes on the ground, her screams piercing the air, the killer calmly gathers the bloody bracelets from the hood and ground. He slings the excess liquid from the gold and deposits them into the opposite cargo pocket.

A higher ranking killer approaches this man, quickly grabbing the man's head by the back of his scalp, pushing his face close

to the two dents the axe blows left on the hood of the vehicle. He pulls the man back, yelling angrily while grasping the subordinate's jaw and face; the attacked man leans down to retrieve some of the bracelets from his pants, not allowed to explain the whole situation. Snatching the offered gold, the man slips it into his breast pocket before forcefully shoving the groveling killer back by his face.

The slightly overweight old woman still struggles in the street, managing to crawl to the curb on knees and elbows and stand. Holding her gushing wrists tight against her stomach under her bosom, my eyes track her path as she runs away; I am curious as to where she will go now in her condition.

A woman's scream reverberates in my small space in the carpet, she screams. "No, no, no!" at the top of her lungs. This voice comes from the rooftop out of view on my immediate left. Compelled to know what is happening on the shorter roof that I had jumped from only about three hours previous, I slowly unfold my razor sharp six clicks knife. Breathlessly I cut three sides of another slit through the rug this time about two by six inches and farther left. Lifting the corner of the freshly cut peep hole, I look down on a distressed familiar face, Em-Mahmood, the mother of Mahmood. Her name comes from a well known custom, the mother and father of a firstborn male child are forever marked in honor of the blessing with new names mirroring their newborn sons.

A uniformed killer stands behind the woman, her arms pinned in his tight bear hug. She screams, "Fear God, fear God, she's not even nine!"

Now a smaller voice screams continually, "Mamma, Mamma, Mamma!"

The roof is built, as usual, with a low five foot tall six inch wide cement retaining wall around its perimeter. Directing my vision further right from the mother, I see her young daughter Nada, about eight and a half years old, laying on her stomach over the middle of the cement wall below me with her feet dangling about a foot off the ground

I know the girl's father well, he evacuated Beirut with the PLO about two weeks ago. She used to go to school with my niece. Her thick black hair hangs full length down the front of the street facing wall, her hands slap the wall from the pain. Nada's pants are loose at her ankles, two killers are busy around the half naked girl; one holds a hand flat on her back to prevent her from falling, the other stands with hands on her waist, struggling to rape her from behind. At first I think it is rape, when I see the growing frustration of the man who seems to have no success behind her, my horror reaches new depths. The beast is intent on sodomizing her. Every so often he removes one hand from Nada's waist to spit in it, bringing the lubrication to his genitals.

Still struggling, the irritated animal screams to the killer holding the girl's mother, Shut her up! I cannot concentrate!"

The man holding Em-Mahmood screams back, "What the hell do you want me to do, I cannot cover her mouth, she would bite me!"

The rapist's eyes spark with rage as he twists back, shaking his finger with gritted teeth at the man behind him holding the mother. Convinced by the silent threat, the killer pulls his knife, slicing the struggling woman's throat open, shouting back, "Are you happy now!" while throwing her to the ground. The guy pushes Em-Mahmood away, she shakes violently in a seizure, blood spraying

as her feet and arms kick and flail in the air. Her murderer jumps to the side in a fright, not willing to dirty his clothes with her overflowing blood.

Seeing enough on this side of the roof, the scene on the other draws me back. The killer rapist still cannot penetrate Nada's behind, she screams still louder for her mother's help, not knowing she is on her own, her mother having just been murdered. The rapist's frustration mounts to dangerous levels, claiming he cannot perform under the stress of her screaming. Reaching down and raising her by the collar, his right hand swings back wide to slap her full on the side of her face; he drops her back down carelessly, letting her head hit the outside cement wall as she almost slides off completely. He grabs her back, repositioning Nada just so to continue in his crime. Moans and choking gasps replace her earlier screams.

The partners' killer who holds Nada's back down with his left hand taps his companion's shoulder with his right, encouraging and offering advise with, "Hey, Safi, relax, relax. You will be able to perform better when you are not stressed; she's not going anywhere."

The rapist straightens, wiping the sweat of his labor from his brow. In earnest he drips spit in his hand, re-lubricating and continuing with deliberation. Twice more until finally he succeeds in entering Nada's anus. The effect of his success is dramatic, the girl's back arches, she raises all the way up even with the force of the hand on her back. I see her eyes, they have rolled back far; only whites showing despite their wide open shock. She faints after being shoved back down, hanging limp; this does not impede the sodomizing rapist who continues to enjoy her lifeless body for several minutes. He shakes in orgasmic pleasure, collapsing in exhaustion over her small body for almost another minute.

The partner pats his back, proudly affirming, “I told you if you just relax you would perform better.”

Not being able to bear any more, I avert my eyes, empty stomach churning but unable to vomit. Returning to my original slit in the rug and to the killing, one sight arrests me—the five Israeli soldiers stand with eyes glued to the same thing I just witnessed. Fifty feet away they stand as if viewing a film; they have watched Nada’s entire rape wordlessly, ignoring the other murders on all sides.

I wish only for an AK-47 or a grenade to finish these base onlookers, their decision not to do anything, to watch a little girl raped by two fully grown men makes them a million times worse than the rapists. Not even one of the Israeli soldiers would forget their orders, use their own judgment to know this is wrong, against basic human nature. I can see them not wanting to stop the killing, but to watch a little girl be raped—at least one of these soldiers must have a young daughter of their own.

I switch window holes again, wanting to check on Nada. The rapist still lays over Nada, his partner taps him impatiently, saying, “Come on, my turn.”

Before rising from the girl, Safi strips the red shirt Nada wears off over her head, using it to wipe away all the blood from his privates. While the killer steps away, he makes a sick comment, “Now you are not going to struggle like I did, now everything is open for you, the way is clear.”

The partner answers back, "Are you crazy, I am not going to step in your filth." He grabs the soiled T-shirt from his friend's hand to wipe away the blood from Nada's behind.

With this clean slate he steps up to his turn, taking the high road, entering the girl in her vagina. This second killer struggles only a minute or two, unlike his partner. Becoming very rough, he lifts Nada up completely in his pounding gyrations. Her head is swinging, I do not know if this movement is from the man's roughness or from her regaining consciousness. Soon there is no question; Nada is awake, beginning to scream loudly in pain, "Ouch, ouch, ouch!"

While reaching her hands to hold her behind. I cannot imagine the pain she is going through.

The man is not phased, he keeps her until finished with his orgasm, pulling her away when it is over, throwing her aside to the cement. Despite her landing Nada rises jumping to her feet, still screaming, "Ouch, ouch, ouch!" Blood streams and sprays from between her legs as she jumps in circles while holding her behind, the only clothing left on her the brown pants and red panties around her ankles. Back-dropped by Nada's jumping and screaming, the second killer takes the red T-shirt back up to clean the blood coating his groin and lower body. Thighs, calves, shoes are soaked in the little girl's blood. The shirt not enough for the job, the first beast kindly retrieves a white towel for his friend from the house; the killer finishes with the towel, pulling up his pants, buckling his belt. Nada sees her dead mother and with one hand in front, one in back, she takes the small steps her fallen pants allow all the way to her mother's side. She screams, "Mamma, Mamma, Mamma!" There is no answer.

The first rapist comes to the girl, softly lifting her pants and underwear back in place. He lifts Nada, holding her hanging from her left bicep and left calf. Walking to the edge of the roof carrying her, he lifts her high, smashing Nada down to the sidewalk below. I cannot see her from this view, but I hear the smashing bone, the weight of impact through the carpet. I see the men exiting the roof, I am doubting if I have the heart to see how Nada has landed. I am more than curious, afraid for her life; shifting views to the original hole in the carpet. I must know if she has survived the fall.

Nada has landed on her right side, her back faces me, there is no sign of life. Tracing her figure, I see that the arm she lays on is bent unnaturally; I assume it is broken. Her hair spreads in a halo on the cement around her head. Even as I examine Nada from this height, I see blood seeping from a hidden head wound through her fanned hair. I nervously wait, hoping she will stir and give some signal she is alive. Three or four minutes pass, the girl begins to regain consciousness, raising her left hand up high, weakly letting it drop back to her side. Again she repeats the hand movement, I am cheered to see she has survived, at the same time I restrain myself from shouting for her to be still. I am gagged by the sure knowledge that the rapist butchers would have me dead in no time if my hiding spot is betrayed. I watch the men below, hoping they will not see the girl reviving; they may come back to finish the job.

A new group of people make their way down the street, a woman follows four butchers who march a young man between them; she screams, “He is only a student, he has never been a soldier!”

I recognize him as Adal Omar, a longtime schoolmate of mine. It is his mother who follows behind. She becomes increasingly

agitated, running in front of the soldiers with clasped hands, pleading, "He is the only son left alive!"

I know Adal Omar has brothers, I have not been able to keep up with the deaths, thus unaware if his mother tells the truth. The war has claimed too many lives. Bothering one of the butchers too brazenly, the man pushes her with a shove to the chest onto the ground. The older matron lands heavily on her butt. The killers guiding her son stop, dividing evenly the space between myself and the five Israeli soldiers posted at the intersection. I sense they have chosen this exact location in order to provide entertainment for their sponsoring Israelis. The way the killers surround my friend Adal can only mean that whatever they plan will end in his death, this much I know.

Two killers split from formation, one heading to the same army truck with the dented hood, the other disappearing to the left of my view. Adal's mother tries to kiss the hand of one of the two left guarding her son, making a last ditch effort to beg his release.

The killer recoils from her attempt, firm to continue as planned. Morbidly intrigued, I am at a loss to predict the killers' next move. The man who headed for the truck now pulls it in a wide U-turn, driving to park next to the rest of the group between the Israeli soldiers and I. The engine is loud as it idles, billowing white smoke. Its tail gate is positioned facing the butchers. The killer has jumped out to join his fellows but the three appear to be waiting for the fourth man who left with the other earlier.

In this pause I cast my gaze back on Nada, relieved to see her laying still with a visibly steady rise and fall of breath. I hear another engine coming down the street, it is the fourth man driving a similar army truck, backing over the bodies littering the main road. He stops the truck five or six feet from the other truck; the tail gates face each other.

Their plans are not secret any more, they are going to murder Adal the old fashioned way. One of the butchers retrieves from the first truck uniformly cut lengths of white rope, the massacre has been minutely premeditated, the ropes cut ahead of time to facilitate the detailed plans. This butcher yells, ordering the victim on his back. Adal resists and the killers struggle to force him down, three beating his face while pinning him to the asphalt as one ties both his arms to one truck, his legs to the opposite.

Adal's mother meanwhile has been fruitlessly beating on the killers' backs as they work, now she throws her body over her son's, desperately fumbling with one hand to untie his limbs. The butchers drive the trucks apart in different directions slowly, my friend raises in the air, his mother still laying over his stomach. My heart goes out to the mother, the one who bore and raised Adal for a happier fate than this. His left arm is first to separate, it drops from his shoulder to the ground, still pulled by the rope attached to the truck. Blood sprays in all directions, covering his mother. She jumps off her son when hit with his blood, wailing to see his dismemberment. She pulls her white head scarf off and waves it in distress. Adal's right arm detaches as she wails. One of the sideline killers, noticing both arms have ripped off, screams for the drivers to stop. One of the drivers climbs down, untying the ropes attached to Adal's arms, tossing the arms with ropes to the side. Both trucks now return to where they came from, the first to the street's side, the other back over the bodies out of sight. The two

killers on foot come to look at their work, walking away from the bleeding young man and his crying mother. They spare her life for now, leaving her to suffer the agony alone.

Kneeling at her son's side, she wraps her arms around his slick armless torso, trying to lift him. Realizing she lacks the strength to carry Adal, she sinks down to rest him in her lap, sitting wet in the blood of her son. I see he is trying to tell his mother something, she listens leaning in to words I cannot hear. Her right hand strokes his hair back again and again, his face showered with her kisses; she knows now as well as I that he will not survive long from the excessive blood lost on the ground. From the pools around his shoulders, it looks as though two thirds of Adal's lifeblood has spilled out.

Checking back on Nada, I am amazed to see her cradled in the arms of an Israeli soldier; the man's back faces me, he strokes the bloody hair from her face as he crosses the street back towards his unit. The ranking Israeli officer on the opposite side angrily gestures at the soldier in the middle of the street with Nada, pointing his finger towards the place where she lay originally. He yells in a language unfamiliar to me, not English, not Arabic, I assume he is speaking Hebrew. The more steps the soldier takes, the angrier the yelling officer becomes, using both hands now to point. When the compassionate soldier reaches the others, the enraged officer strikes his arms, trying to force him to drop Nada. Almost losing her at this unexpected move, he tightens his grip, bringing her body and his forearms close to his chest. The situation is personal at this point, the soldier disobeying direct orders from a ranking officer. I think perhaps the soldier may have a daughter or sister Nada's age, perhaps feeling she has suffered enough after the unspeakable atrocities committed against her.

The officer and soldier lock in a physical battle of wills, the former trying to wrestle his soldier's fists down to release the girl's body; the soldier whips away in a 180 degree turn. Having had enough, the officer calls in the other three to help pry the man's arms away; the incensed man yanks Nada by her hair out of the restrained man's arms. The man drags her a ways down the sidewalk, I see she is conscious, her broken arm raising as she is pulled over the ground. Casting the girl thirty feet or so away, the officer stomps back to tie up the rest of the spectacle.

The soldier is behaving outrageously, he has lost control, still straining against the other men to reach Nada. The officer barks an order, a white zip tie is produced that is used to tie the struggling soldier's hands behind his back. Once tied, he is shoved into the opened jeep door, the vehicle doubling as an indefinite containing room.

This scene stirs me, I remember the promise of protection I made to Rola; like the soldier, I should be fighting for her instead of hiding like a coward in this carpet. A crazy idea forms in my head. I should jump the roofs to her house, the chances are slim I will make it alive; but I must try. The hundreds of butchers running rampant in the camp are killing every moving thing even as I contemplate. I am torn, I will not hesitate to die for Rola if I know my death will save her life, I would jump the roofs in a heartbeat. The problem is that if I do die and Rola is hiding safe, then my sacrifice will hurt her more. She and her mother might have escaped before the attack, I have no way of knowing. The conflicting ideas and my lack of information

forces my pragmatism to win out; it is dusk and growing dimmer, I will wait until dark to make my move, my odds at survival would be higher in the cover of nightfall.

Emerging from the reverie of my plans, I notice from the first peep hole a killer sitting on the curb directly across the way, busily cutting four or five foot lengths from a large coil of rope. Already having witnessed what they use the ropes for, I am confused why they would need so many; quartering is an inefficient killing process. Women holding children's hands run to and fro between the alleys and side streets, I am encouraged to see evidence of life.

From the road near the cinema I see a large group of people coming to the intersection. Thirty armed killers surround forty to fifty elderly men, women, and children, stopping them to the side of where the four Israeli soldiers watch. The killer sitting on the curb struggles with the bulky arm load of rope he brings to throw near the group, each soldier grabs a handful. The killer who seems to be in command stands in front of the innocent people, walkie talkie in hand. He announces that the men in the group will be tied for their own safety. He repeats the phrase, "Don't try anything stupid, you will be shot if you try to run away," three to five times.

The officer screams, "I want the men on my right, the women and children on my left!" standing lookout for his busy men and watching for anything suspicious as they bind up the men's arms and ankles. The scene is before me as an open book, I can read ahead; the intention of the butchers leaves no doubt in my mind that there is no safety for these people.

While the old men are tied up, the more subtle action between husbands and wives, mothers and children is breaking my heart.

Women cry, wiping tears away with the ends of their head scarves. Some pat their men's shoulders, talking to each other between the short gap dividing them. Small children cling to their mother's dresses, not knowing enough to be scared of the busy killers, shyly hiding from view in the dress fabric, playing a kind of hide and seek. The looks on the people's faces leads me to believe they have not yet discovered the full intention of the killers, despite the dead bodies littering the street, hope keeps them docile.

When all the men are bound, the killers move from around the group to stand at their officer's side. I cannot hear in the commotion, but I see the officer speaking into his walkie talkie, putting it up to his ear several times. He laughs at the last transmission, holstering the device on his side. He feels the time is ripe for a speech, saying, "I just want you to know that all of you are going to die, but first I want you to know why. For years past you have destroyed our country, you have divided our cities, you have ruled the way you saw fit. You are like a disease in our country and in our society, the only way this country will ever recover is for you to disappear off the face of the earth, not by letting you go so you can come back. So we are going to make sure, at this time, at this place, that all of you are going to hell."

This said, the women break the air with cries, many screaming, "Mercy, mercy!"

One of the women in front pleads, "Please, can you at least get the children out of the line!" as she pulls her small daughter behind her.

The same man in charge takes a couple steps to scream loudly in her face, "Why, so they can grow up and come to destroy our country again?! We are not taking this chance tonight!"

This said, he falls back to the rear of his officers, ordering them to shoot. Hell breaks loose in the spray of bullets from thirty killers' guns. Not being able to take the sight, in the pounding barrage of open fire I sink slowly to my knees in the carpet, eyes closed. It is quiet after about two minutes and I stand to see the heaps of bodies. One woman stands from among the slain, her hand presses against the bullet wound in her neck. Blood sprays through her fingers as she staggers towards the officer. The commanding butcher pulls his handgun, shooting her square between the eyes. She crumples at his feet, he steps over her, picking through the other bodies, emptying first one clip, then another into any of the survivors, shooting anyone still breathing.

The pile of bodies hemorrhage on the street, together they create thick streams of blood that run between and past the murderers. These trample the flow underfoot in army boots, desecrating the silent witnesses.

Watching the blood passing my hiding place, I think, *I have seen so much blood in my life, but I have never seen this much blood in one place. This is truly what they mean when they say blood bath.*

Another Jeep with a long antennae comes rolling down the hill from Sports City, stopping behind the already parked vehicle with the four Israelis on guard in front. The uniformed passenger jumps out, walkie talkie in hand, making straight for the ranking officer of the four; he pulls the man aside down the sidewalk. They walk as far as Nada's body and after a brief consultation the new soldier heads back to the Jeep housing the prisoner Israeli, letting the crying man out while pulling a knife from his right pocket to cut the zip tie off him. The two walk to the middle of the street and back two or three times, the crying soldier being comforted by the new one, his arm around the other's shoulder as the two talk. It looks as though the back up is smoothing over the trouble, the newcomer leads the soldier to the second Jeep. It turns around with its new cargo, returning the way it came, back up the hill.

The butcher in charge of the blood flow running in the street, the man who recently gave a speech, makes his way to the Israeli officer in charge of the blocked intersection. The officer offers the approaching butcher a cigarette from a pack he pulls from his breast pocket. He lights the accepted smoke for the man; the two begin a congenial conversation that lasts ten minutes or more, broken by laughter.

The friendly discussion is interrupted by a yell from the farthest Israeli from them, alerting the butcher in charge that an elderly gentleman who has risen from the pile of dead in the street is escaping. The old man in black shirt and slacks runs for his life, darting away to the right towards Sabra camp.

The head killer runs after him, past the point where I can see. A few minutes later he returns, towing the old man by his shirt front. The butcher stops between my position and the Israeli soldiers', calling one of his men to bring him the cutters. Meanwhile the butcher loses no time, punching the old man's face sixteen or seventeen times before the man returns, handing the head butcher heavy metal snips.

Most of the killers are on break, smoking and watching the latest action from side groups. They are worn out from their work. Five or six killers have joined their leader, surrounding the

struggling old man who is pulling his tightly clenched fists away from the scissors. They mean to cut his fingers off. The lead killer is visibly angry at the old man's trick, wanting to punish this one slowly and leisurely. The old man is not begging for his life like the others, actually inciting his captors by spitting in their faces, cursing them all the while. Eventually they wrest the man to the ground; three killers holding his body while others force his fist flat on the pavement. The cutters are brought, the old man howls in excruciating pain as each finger is easily cut off at the base. After the first two he goes limp, still screaming but no longer resisting. First one hand, then the other is stripped of its digits.

Finished with their fun, the killers let the man up, dismissing him from them; he has survived the shooting, he has survived the punishment for his survival and they ask him to leave. The old man refuses to leave, pushing himself up by his palms, standing and bleeding from ten taps running blood, while continuing his tirade.

"Cowards! You would have never made it to this camp if the PLO were still here!"

The head butcher speaks for the rest, his anger mounting again after the surprise of the old man's refusal to escape with his life, saying, "You need to get your facts straight, I will tell you who is the coward, the real coward is your leader Yasser Arafat. He is the one who took the soldiers, running away from Beirut like a dog with its tail tucked between its legs! We are not cowards, we just finally have the opportunity to kill you all like dogs. You see, we are not cowards!"

The old man pushes further, yelling back, "I promise you one day the PLO will return to Beirut, then we will do exactly to you what you are doing to us now! We will rape your women, kill your children, insult your elderly!"

The butcher in charge explodes in sarcastic laughter, rearing his head back. His back facing me, I cannot see the butcher's expression, but I can tell the old man is getting under his skin. Shaking his finger, the butcher scolds, "Okay, the PLO might return, but I promise you one thing, we are going to kill you all before we leave here!"

Now the old man digs deep, saying as he holds his stunted hands in front of them, "You see these hands without fingers now, you have made it easier now, these hands will go easy when I stick them in your Mamma!"

Hearing this, I know the old man has his death wish. The only reason I can see why he insists on dying here when he had the chance to leave is maybe wanting to join the family he just lost to these butchers.

The butcher in charge steps out, grabbing the man's throat, shouting, "Did I hear you correctly? Did I hear you say you were going to stick your hands in my Mamma? Don't you know who's my Mamma, she's the Virgin Mary!"

While he grasps the man's throat, the head butcher orders his men to hold the man still from behind, to keep his feet still. Another killer is instructed to chop off all the barefoot man's toes with an axe. Hitting each foot twice to complete the task.

The now fingerless and toeless man still stands defiantly next to his severed toes, yelling, "We still are going to go to your homes and do worse than this to you! I'm going to search in those homes until I find your Mamma, when I do I am going to please her well;

I am going to make sure that she is pleased with my performance!"

The head butcher bristles, yelling like a drill sergeant in the old man's face, "You are still talking about my Mamma! I'm going to shut you up, but I'm not going to kill you because I know that's what you want. You are going to survive even if you are the only one in these two camps!"

Ordering the killers to hold his head, the head butcher tries to pry open the man's mouth; the old man clenches his teeth hard, forcing the butcher to use the butt of his large knife, breaking all the man's front teeth away. Reaching deep with his knife, the butcher slices away the tongue, throwing it down next to the toes. Now a bleeding gibbering mess, the old man is released again to the sound of scornful laughter.

The head butcher mocks, "Do you believe this clown? He is probably still trying to cuss my mother!"

All the killers gathered around joining in the laughter, watching the defeated man walk away on his heels, hands held dripping in front as he hobbles. Nothing more to say or do, the old man leaves, probably to bleed to death alone; there is no need for him to stay as entertainment for the butchers. I am sorry to see the man not get his way, denied the chance to die with honor.

The sun is down and I can just barely see the growing mounds of dead in the streets, spreading as far as I can see in the dusk. I hear far-off screams from the streets behind my rooftop, still seeing killers in the dim light going house to house, busy finishing off the last survivors.

Drawing back to remember my own condition in the carpet, I am trapped. My feet are numb but I cannot bear to relieve their aching by sitting because of the vomit. The smell of it by this time is rancid, the heat mingling this with my sweat in the stuffy prison. My only comfort is the thought that Rola must be safe; I have convinced myself she is fine. These thoughts alone keep my aching knees from collapsing. I am extremely dehydrated, not even having enough saliva to swallow. Through my suffering, my mind has convinced my heart that there will be a happy ending, this alone sustains me.

I strain my eyes through the flap on the left, trying to cut through the darkness to see something of Rola's house four or five hundred feet away. Taller houses block my view, my thoughts shift; for Rola's sake I begin thinking of God, thinking of praying for her safety. I cannot bring myself to this, not wanting to pray to that God to save someone. If he is a good God then he should do what a good God would do. He should not be asked or prayed to in order to save the people.

I have been hearing all my life that God is here and there, that he is everywhere; if this is true he must be here, if he is here then that is worse. If he is real then he is watching all this killing, if he is watching and does nothing then he approves of it. He should have the power to stop it if he wants; you cannot be God without any power. If he were powerless, then he would be like me in this carpet, helpless to stop this massacre against my people. God must hate us for some reason, to allow all this killing. I have been instructed that this god knows our thoughts, that he watches and orders the steps of each man. I reach a conclusion: God must be out of the picture here. I consider my faith destroyed.

I find myself whispering in the carpet, "Please Rola, please Rola, be okay, be fine. Don't let them hurt you."

My thoughts are cut short by gunfire from the end of the camp towards Rola's house. The butchers are transformed in the darkness into killers, now using more bullets than blades and axes. I am amazed, surprised they are finding more people to kill without any light in the camp. There has not been any electricity in the camps since the Israeli army's invasion.

Hearing firing from this side scares me. I have not seen Rola now for hours. For me this is a lifetime, every passing minute in the carpet is an hour. My hopes that the killers would leave with the coming darkness is shattered. Any second now I feel I will collapse, my feet are shaking, barely able to hold my body. I am so thirsty.

Small flashlights bob in the distance. I hear screams of women and sounds of people being dragged from back houses to main streets. Sprays of bullets silence the screams. I do not understand why the killers are bothering to bring people to the streets before shooting them. All of a sudden the Israeli Jeep's lights flip on, blinding me temporarily. I think first they must want a better view, seconds later I see I am wrong; the Jeep turns around and climbs the hill to the base at Sports City.

A few minutes pass and I hear muted bangs of fire works from the hill, to my horror the sky lights up again but this time artificially with continuous flares. The sky over both Sabra and Shatila camps turns to daylight. My last hopes are shredded, with the aid of Israeli flares the people of the camp are going to have a long night. The flares are evidence that this massacre has been planned ahead, the Lebanese guerillas, or the Lebanese Christian Phalangist militia, and the Israeli army are working in conjunction to wipe out both camp's populations. The flares tell me that the Israeli army is being a great facilitator to thc killing butchers. The light from the flares is like making the clock turn backward to the daylight. This brings them joy, to us it brings more killing.

With an indefinite time period ahead, my plans to jump the roofs to Rola's house are canceled. I do not know how much longer I can keep myself from collapsing; I know that even so, I am better off than those being slaughtered in the streets, precarious as my position may be. One glance from a butcher and I face the same fate as the murdered. I do not fear for my own life, what is keeping me sane is the promise I made to the woman that means the world to me. The one thing striking fear in my heart is whether Rola has been able to keep her promise to me, if she has been able to stay safe. I refuse to accept the thought that something has harmed her during this insane and random binge of killing.

I hear voices coming from the street bordering the left of my building, I see the tips of two killer's military boots. They are sitting on the sidewalk straight below me, their bodies cropped by the rooftop. Women still scream in the distance but over this I have no trouble hearing every word from the two in the stillness. Sound travels clearer in the summer night and I am privy to every whisper.

Soft light bounces off what I see of the men, they are lighting cigarettes; I can smell the tobacco wafting up straight to where I stand about twelve feet above. The smell awakes my craving to light up as well. The cigarettes and lighter in my back pocket are no use to me if I value my life. Trying to light a cigarette now would reveal my hiding place. This danger barely holds me back;

I will do anything for a cigarette, willingly trade an arm or leg for the relief. A cigarette not being an option, I turn my focus to the killer's conversation.

One of the two says to the other, "Man, what a day today. I feel like my penis is going to fall off," bragging of his rapes. "I had sex with about thirteen of those young girls today!"

Both laugh, the other banters back, "Well I had about seventeen of them." He goes further than the first, divulging that, "You know what, I found out that to have sex with those young girls with their parents watching is the ultimate rush."

His companion replies, "Man, you are sick."

The other sounds shocked as he asks, "Don't tell me you haven't tried it today!"

"Of course I did, but I didn't think it was the ultimate rush."

The first killer continues, "You know what happened? One of them died when me and George were having sex with her."

Skeptical, the other asks, "Died from having sex with you two guys?"

"Yeah, that's what I said."

The skeptical one asks again "How old was this girl?"

"I didn't see her birth certificate, but I would say six or seven."

Putting on an air of decency, the other replies, "Well I didn't go that young, I go nine years old and above."

"Well you should try the younger ones, they are really amazing."

"No, I'll leave those to you." Is his prudish answer.

Continuing the debate, the first killer says, "Look at it this way, my penis is fine, that tells you something." Meaning, I assume, that younger is better.

He asks, “How many of them do you think we killed today?”

The other decent one answers, “I don’t know how many, I wasn’t counting, but I would estimate probably two thousand.”

This same man asks the first, “How many of them did you personally kill today?”

“I’m not sure, forty or fifty of them.”

Reflecting the same question back on the other, the second answers, “About twenty, twenty-five.”

His friend exclaims, “You have been lazy!”

“Man I thought there would be a lot more people than this in these camps!”

What the other man says now in a Beirut accent scares the living daylights out of me, “Oh don’t worry, we are just getting started. All those streets in front and back of here we haven’t touched yet.”

The first tells the other, “When we start with those other homes in the narrow streets, I bet you we are going to find beautiful young girls there! I advise you to fix your penis right now, go get some treatment or something if you want to get busy.”

Laughing at this the second cackles, “Oh don’t worry, I am going to perform even if my penis falls off!”

Listening to this disturbing conversation, my suspicions are confirmed; these butchers have not yet quenched their thirst for rape or mass murder. They still thirst for more blood, hunger for more killing. I now regret that I gave up my handgun to the Israelis. Now I wish I could shoot these two fiends, even if I die in the attempt. If I died at least I would save some young girls from rape and some elderly from death or torture.

These feelings are pointless, the hosting Israelis made sure to sweep out all weapons in the camps, just to ensure the butchers' safety. I am more deeply convinced now that this massacre has been planned ahead. I have figured out the order of affairs: first get rid of the PLO from Beirut, then get rid of the personal weapons in the camps, then get rid of the people of the camps by killing them all. It seems to me that only the devil and the Israelis could hatch an idea like this.

What is more shameful is that the Israeli army makes pretense of keeping their hands clean, bringing in the Lebanese Christian Phalangists to do the dirtiest job in the universe. Now the Israeli army can deny any wrong doing in Sabra and Shatila, the blame simply falling on their friendly mercenaries, despite the fact that while all this is happening both camps are under total Israeli control.

My gut tells me this plan will succeed, the Israeli government convincing the world that they had nothing to do with the massacre. This planning ahead is meticulous, each base covered, including foreign relations. If what I am forecasting is really to happen, it can mean one thing only, that the blood of the victims of Sabra and Shatila camps will be lost forever between the Israeli government and the Lebanese Christian Phalangists.

As an educated young man seeing the slaughter of my people before my eyes, one question surfaces in my mind. How could the people who suffered the torture and the massacres during the second World War at the Nazi's hands now turn around and do worse than what was done to them in the concentration camps?

The events here in Sabra and Shatila are by far exceedingly

worse than what they have suffered. As I stand still hidden in the carpet, I think the experience with the Nazis must have been a lesson in killing and rape that the Israelis learned well. I see the deeds of the middle man, the ones doing the actual killing, but personally I think middle men are not to be blamed for a simple reason: if someone owns a mad dog, that owner is responsible for its leashing and unleashing. Common knowledge blames the possessor of the mad animal for any injury it causes. The Israeli government therefore is at fault for unleashing its dogs on both camps of Sabra and Shatila.

Two major questions come from these deep contemplations of mine one, what kind of *hate* is that? Two, what kind of *revenge* is that?

CHAPTER SIX

The Smell of Blood in the Air

Not even able to estimate what time of night it is, I am certain that the flares shot from the Israeli army's base on the hill illuminate both camps brightly. In intervals, the night returns between flares, every five or six minutes night turns back to day; my eyes are confused, struggling to adjust to this strange flux.

In the zenith of the last flare I see a handful of killers loitering on the roof of the house straight ahead, on a break from their gruesome duty it seems in the young night. Their presence unnerves me, the even plane between us may reveal to them the flares' reflection in my eyes through the hole in the carpet. Knowing I am witnessing history, the risk of keeping my eyes wide open is worth it. Something moves in the pile of dead to the left in the open street, I adjust my eyes to see an older man, light flashing off his bald head, struggling to sit down among the corpses. He is unable to find a stable seat.

He must have passed out or played dead until the right moment to show signs of life. I notice his right arm is missing, he wobbles while adjusting himself with his left, finally sitting. Now going one step further, the man pushes on a body under him, trying to stand. Not only his right hand is severed but his right leg is nearly so, dangling from above the knee, attached only by a few stray nerves. He hobbles bleeding from both stumps to a nearby house, he leans his only hand on the wall, supporting himself while jerking his right leg off by stepping on the dangling foot with the left. Now free of the impediment, hc slowly moves an inch at a time on the one leg, twisting back and forth to propel himself forward.

The lounging killers on the roof watch, one pulls his handgun to finish the old man. He is stopped short by one of his companions. I cannot hear, but it seems the consensus is that the man should be left to live in this condition if he can. I am surprised the old man has survived this long, I hope he will die—only more suffering will meet him if he lives beyond this point. Measuring by my standard, I would not want to live after losing an arm and a leg.

Not having traveled far, the old man slides to sit against the wall, pulling the green cotton shirt from over his head. He tears the fabric in strips; tying tourniquets aided by his teeth around first his arm, then his leg. I understand his natural desire to preserve what is left of his life, at whatever quality. Past this move I

wonder what he will do, the only two hospitals are Gaza Hospital between Sabra and Shatila, and Akka Hospital located in the South end of Shatila, in the area of Beer-Hassan.

Gaza Hospital was not much help even before the massacre, the inhabitants there are as doomed as all the rest of us. As far as Akka Hospital, I learn later that it was attacked before the camps. The killers entered the building to end the patient's lives, murder the doctors and then rape and kill the female nurses. This elderly man's chances of survival are close to nothing.

Training my eyes on his halting movements, I see the man attempting to stand again for six or seven minutes. Quitting finally, he sits still for a moment before biting and pulling off the fabric tourniquets he only recently tied. He sits bleeding, conceding, I think, to accept death like a man, with dignity. I still watch, and after a few minutes I see the old man shaking. Soon his soul will be released from the wounded body. I glance back to the rooftop, the killers have vacated. Under the dimming light of the dying flares I strain to catch any sound, there is none. No screams, nothing. The sense that now is the time for my escape rises up in me, before the Israelis shoot new flares. I decide to make my move, pulling the rug away.

I stagger weakly on numb feet towards the back of the roof, weaving through the hanging laundry to check each side of the building for any witnesses in the streets. Seeing nothing but dead bodies, I make for the back of the roof, the exit point of my escape. I breathe freely for the first time in hours, filling my lungs not with fresh clean air but with the strong smell of fresh blood.

Slowly I climb over the rooftop's edge, hanging full length

from my hands before dropping the remaining five feet as quietly as possible. Now on street-level, I creep along, careful not to step on any debris that might make a sound. The butchers are all over. I skim the houses on the side of the street, walking sideways with my back touching the walls. I trip on the strewn bodies in the darkness, stepping in liquid that can only be blood. Having progressed about a thousand feet from where I dropped down, I hear the sound of flares. Soon the sky lights again and I find myself exposed in the street. There is no returning. I no longer feel safe and decide to run the rest of the distance.

As I dodge the bodies I can see a little ahead that the street is clear. It is a place where the butchers have not yet reached. I am distracted by the muffled cry of a woman wailing over a pile of dead, she is a little ways down a side street. A small flashlight lights the area where she kneels. I do not hesitate to alter my path, wanting to check to see if she needs anything. This is the first chance I have had to offer any help to my people.

Noiselessly I approach her from behind, whispering, "Are you okay?"

The woman jumps to her feet, shining the light on my face as she backs away fearfully. She thinks I am one of the killers, even though I am dressed in civilian clothes unlike the killers who wear uniforms. I cannot blame her for not trusting anyone.

Wanting to calm her fears, I whisper again, "I'm a survivor, just like yourself."

The middle aged woman's knees are bloody from where she had knelt by the bodies, her brown velvet robe dark and dripping. She takes a few steps towards me, flashlight still shining in my

face. She is incredulous, telling me, "You are lucky you survived, I didn't know anybody survived. God must be looking after you."

Aiming the light to the pile of bodies, she says, "Look, this is my family. This is my oldest daughter Fatamah," now she shows me an eight or nine-month old baby on the ground next to the daughter, explaining, "this is her son, my grandson."

Looking at the baby, I see his rib cage is smashed; the infant was killed with one stomp. The woman continues her introduction, indicating a young girl with a slit throat about thirteen-years old.

Tears drop from her cheeks as she tells me, "This is my younger daughter Nesreen." A sixty-year old man is spotlighted next, "this is my husband Khaliel, we have been married thirty-eight years."

I do not know how her husband died, I cannot distinguish if the two wounds in his chest are from bullets or knife stabs. A woman with an arm cut off at the wrist and a slit throat, aged about forty, is the woman's sister. I imagine she wore jewelry on that wrist, remembering the other woman who lost both hands for the bangles.

I have to cut the woman short, I see she does not need physical help she needs emotional help. I have no time to waste as empathetic as I may feel. I hurry her with, "Okay, I see them."

She tearfully exclaims, "They are all here, all my family. THEY ARE ALL HERE!"

"You had better lower your voice," I warn, scanning the streets for any movement, "I am sure they are still hiding around here."

She screams, "WHY DO I CARE! I WANT THEM TO HEAR ME! WHAT ARE THOSE COWARDS GOING TO DO, ARE THEY GOING TO KILL ME? I DON'T WANT TO LIVE ANYWAY, SOMEBODY KILL ME PLEASE!"

I cannot help calm her down, she is a danger to herself and to me as well. Truly I feel sorry for this older woman, she has lost all of her family. I do not blame her for wanting to commit suicide by the same hands that took her loved ones.

I know I must keep moving so I tell her, "I'm going to have to go, would you like to come with me?"

She says, "Son, you don't understand what I said, you are still young, run for your life. I am as good as dead."

Released by these words I continue running, passing the killing line, leaving the dead bodies behind. Now feeling a little more secure I slow to a walk, consumed by thoughts of Rola, of how I can get back to her house. I have escaped the thickest area of killing but all I can think of now is how to get back there. I know definitely that the killers are there on the main street where Rola's house is and I will not make it if I try to get through right now.

Walking the desolate streets, I wonder how extensive the massacre really is, if it is possible that all the people in the camps have been murdered. I am alone; the woman I just left and myself, I feel I am the only survivor. I stop in my tracks, turning around one hundred and eighty degrees. I have to go back, my heart will not let me be a coward and let Rola suffer without me.

Retracing my steps towards death street, my mind tells me this idea is the worst in the history of bad ideas. I do not care. I switch off the practical advice in my head. Rola is the inspiration that draws me back to an uncertain fate. She is worth far more to me than my own life.

I begin tripping again on the dead bodies, walking in plain sight with my heart pounding in my chest I wait for a killer to

jump out of hiding to slaughter me. For some reason this does not concern me, not feeling brave, just not caring. I must get to Rola.

On the way I see a lighted house, curious I go closer to the open door. Someone is moving inside, long shadows on the walls. Now within twenty-five feet I see a figure pass the doorway—a uniformed man! I throw myself down next to a dead woman, playing dead while keeping my eyes on the house. One man in the house has a strong handheld floodlight. Clearly I see other men in the house searching through closets, throwing clothes, lifting mattresses. They must be looking for money or jewelry; not only killers, but thieves too.

The killer-thieves leave to ransack the house next door. Three killers pass within feet of me on their treasure hunting mission, I hear one say to the next, "Those bastards are not as poor as they look."

I am in the thick of the action, knowing that if there are three killers here, there must be many more nearby. While the men are occupied in the new house I begin army crawling towards the main street. Looking left towards Rola's house, I see a peppering of lighted cigarettes in the hands of sixty or seventy killers who sit together on the curb of the main street sharing stories. It is clear now that it is impossible for me to make it alive to her house, I decide to retreat from this cursed street to the middle of the camp, where I had been safer before returning here.

I crawl away, playing dead periodically when I hear danger coming. Now coming to the end of the narrow road, I stand and start running. I keep running until I reach my brother's house in the middle of Shatila; the door is open. The killers have not made it this far but I know it is only a matter of time.

First thing I do is head for the bathroom. Finding a container half full of water; I slack my thirst, bringing handfuls of the brown stale water to my mouth. My jeans and tee shirt are caked with blood and dirt from crawling so I strip off my clothes and stand naked on the cement floor. Four green towels hang neatly on a stand, I grab one, dipping it in the water and cleaning the blood from me. Now cleansed I walk to my brother's room, opening the two folding doors of his closet. I choose from the neatly folded clothes fresh pants, a shirt and some tennis shoes. Now clothed, I begin searching for food but there is nothing.

I long for sleep, this is not possible with the killers liable to come at any moment. I leave the house, returning to the street, walking farther away for about ten minutes.

Far off I see a large group of people standing in the middle of the street. Shocked and overjoyed to see that many people alive on their feet, I walk towards them. Right away I ask them, "How far have the killers gotten?"

One woman from the crowd answers, "They haven't been here yet. We are very scared, we do not know where to go or what to do."

Their arms are full of bed sheets stuffed with pillows and clothes, in hopes I am sure of finding some refuge. I ask, "Why don't you leave the camp?"

An older gentleman tells me, "We were told that the Israelis have sealed all the exita. They are not allowing anybody to leave. I think they want us dead, they don't want anybody to survive this."

I warn them, "Listen to me people, those butchers are not done yet. I heard them, they are planning more killings. Find a safe place to hide."

In order to emphasize what I just said, I relate the story of what I had overheard the two killers say who sat below me just before I left the rooftop.

I stop the story when I realize I am only heightening the people's fear. Another woman in the group calls out, "I don't know where we should hide. It is a small camp. They are going to find us no matter where we hide."

I have nothing to say to this, I know she is right. There is no such thing as a safe place in this camp. I know first hand that the killers will go from home to home, not sparing anyone. They are trained executioners.

For some reason I remember the underground shelter, saying aloud, "The shelter—it's safe!"

Another older woman says, "I'm not sure if it's safe or not, but at least if we are going to die we will die all together."

There is a silent agreement to try the shelter, it is below ground level and there is a chance the killers might miss it. We all walk to the shelter in a group. On arrival I step up and open the heavy metal door, helping the elderly ones down the steps first. Now that all of us are downstairs, people feel their way to claim spots, some producing candles from their escape kits, all settling in as a matter of business.

Candles dimly light the room, the scene reminds me of Rola. I announce a pressing question, "Does anyone have a cigarette?"

An older man, probably in his early seventies, passes me a pack of French Getan, without filters. He says in a grandfatherly manner, "Keep the whole pack, I have another."

Sitting to the side against the shelter wall, I take two deep drags, it is good. I did not even have to trade an arm or a leg.

As I rest, the people hammer me with questions, one woman asking, "Are they killing only men?"

I refrain from answering as another asks, "How many do you think they have killed?"

These are only a few of the many similar inquiries, I decide to keep silent, knowing whatever I say can only scare them to death. I tell them only, "My advise to you is not to go to Dalal El Mograbi street," which is the main street, "just because there is going to be more killing in the daytime." I want to warn them that the danger will not cease in the morning, not having to go into details to get the point across.

I break loose from the group to wander over to where Rola's mattress used to lay. I lay down in the same spot, wanting to feel close to her. In this moment I feel peace, laying thinking of her; hoping she is safe. I cannot explain why I have no doubt she is safe, my mind and heart will not accept the alternative. The idea of facing life without her is unbearable. In this fragile peace of mind I slip into sleep on the cement floor, my arm serving as a pillow for my head.

Friday, September 17th

I awake peacefully from a deep sleep on the second day of the massacre to see an empty room. Looking around, I see the people I brought pressed together in a corner. It looks like they have not slept for fear—screams from outside the shelter terrify them—none having risked opening the door to see what is happening on the ground. The thought of being discovered, of being slaughtered at any moment has not allowed anyone to relax.

I shake myself awake and walk slowly up the stairs to the door. Lifting the lid just a crack, I squint into the morning light. I see people are standing close in the streets, I hear screams in the background. They are all looking straight ahead to some spot out of my view, women hold hands over their mouths in the characteristic pose of horror known all too well in the camps. Being reassured by the sight of people alive at least, I lift the heavy door overhead, and step out to ask an elderly couple nearby what was going on.

Both of them try to answer at once, the couple looks at each other and the man waves a hand at his spouse, "Hush, let the two men talk!"

I wait for him to answer and he finally explains that in the early morning when the sun was first rising, some survivors came to tell them that the killing was over…that it was safe. People from the side and back streets had poured out to sift through the bodies, looking for family members and friends. It was a trick. The killers must have pulled out temporarily somewhere, perhaps to their hosting Israeli base up the hill in Sports City. When the streets were full the butchers descended again, piling fresh dead on the existing piles.

These people outside the shelter are waiting nervously for the return of those who went to check the bodies from last night's carnage. Some who went had escaped back to inform the others that it was not safe. Nowhere in the camp was safe. There was nowhere to go.

The old man's wife cuts in, "I'm very scared and worried!"

The old man replies to this meanly, saying, "We are all going to die. They are going to kill us all. Why should we be worried, it's a matter of hours."

I scrutinize the man closely, he has already given up, has resigned himself to death. I look for an exit from this conversation. This man is not making me or his wife feel any better. I back away to the side of the crowd to join them in waiting for whatever would come next.

I light one of the Getan cigarettes given to me by the old man in the shelter, smoking nervously while waiting for a word from the main street.

Halfway through the cigarette a young man, probably around fifteen or sixteen years old, runs through us screaming, "Run for your lives, they are walking this way! The killers are walking this way!"

Everyone scatters in the opposite direction except the first old man I talked to, he truly has given up. The man sits down on the asphalt, legs crossed under him; his frantic wife pulls on the back of his collar trying to make him stand and run with her.

The seventy-something year old is unresponsive, unwilling to flee, he only throws her hand off, screaming, "Run for your life woman!"

The woman yells back, "I'm not leaving without you. You have been my husband over fifty years!"

This scene catches my heart, I pause before running, watching the woman lift her skirts to sit in the same manner by her husband's side. They look sadly at each other, he wraps his arm around her shoulder as her head sinks to rest on his chest. Tears come to my eyes, watching these old people decide to die together.

I run back to the shelter, shouting urgently down the stairs for them all to come up quickly. I stand to the side as they stream out, directing them to run away from the main street. I am losing time

for my own escape but cannot leave them without at least alerting them. When the last person comes out I run down to make sure no one is left behind, the space is empty.

I catch up with the group, we run together for ten minutes or so until we reach an open field called Ard-Jalool (Jalool's land). This land is used as a kind of carnival grounds during the annual Aleid celebration, the largest Muslim celebration all over the world. This same field used to double as a soccer field for my school friends and I. We all sit down together in a circle in the middle of the field, from here we can see in all directions. This way one of us will be able to see death coming.

Now outside the main structures of the camps, I see the Gaza hospital building, about three or four hundred feet away, between Sabra and Shatila camps.

Out here in the middle of nowhere, all of us wonder what will happen next, waiting to die, waiting to live…just waiting. There are thirty-eight of us, mostly older people, women and children, only four or five younger men like myself. While we wait to be discovered by the Israeli army or the Lebanese Christian Phalangists, each minute that passes is like an hour. A dispute rises up, the women debate which group is more likely to find us first.

A woman speaks up, stating to everyone's agreement that, "If the Israelis find us first they will hold us as hostages, then they will pass us to the butchers for slaughter."

We wait for a long time, sitting here without food or water. Children begin to complain loudly of hunger and thirst, their mothers try to muffle their cries. We are all fearful that they may give our position away prematurely. I feel for the children, they are asking for such simple things; they cannot understand the situation.

While the moms deal with the children, an old man stands up, pointing towards the camp shouting, "Look, look!"

Our attention follows his finger, a woman trudges across the field to us with an awkward gait, a small child clutched to her chest. From the way she is walking it looks like she may be injured. Our collective gaze is locked on her as she stops a couple of feet from us. Silent tears course down the woman's face; blood stains her dark green dress from her thighs down, the child in her arms is a girl, maybe two years old.

I assume the crying woman is in her late twenties, there is no scarf on her head, her feet are bare. An older woman from the circle takes the little girl, the mother cries harder, wailing, "They killed my husband, they killed my two little children right in front of my eyes! They gathered around them, chopping them with axes like animals! They have no mercy, just two tiny children, three and five years old!"

Escalating to a scream, she continues, "My two children, they didn't do anything to them, they didn't hurt anybody, just two little innocents!" Looking around the crowd as if searching for an exclamation, the hysterical woman asks, "Can someone tell me why this is happening to us?"

Four women approach to comfort the woman, holding her, stroking her hair, patting her back. One of the four says, "You are bleeding between your legs." The injured woman is ashamed, after looking down at her dress her head remains down.

One of the comforting women puts a hand out to lift the fallen chin, looking her in the eyes, saying, "It's okay, there is nothing to be ashamed of, everybody here in the group understands, God

understands. Lift your head up high, you just lost your husband and children. The whole idea of this massacre is to make us ashamed, to lower our heads to the ground; but we are not going to do that, we are going to keep our chins up. We are going to show those bastards that we will die with our heads up.

"You know what? They are the ones who should feel shame, for murdering women and children. They are the ones who should fear God. Believe me, God will not forget what is happening here, one day the Israelis and those Phalangists are going to face much worse than what they are doing to us at this moment."

The crying woman wipes her tears away with her hands, composing herself after the wise encouragement of the old woman. Another woman sitting on the ground passes her a white hand towel to wipe her legs with, she grabs the towel, wiping what blood she can from under her skirt. Looking up at us who have followed her movements with sorrowful eyes, she for some reason feels a need to explain, maybe from pride.

She begins crying again when she tells us, "This was the only way to have them spare my daughter's life." She continues with tears flowing from an open tap, "Eleven of them raped me, taking turns. When they were done one of them stuck their army boot inside me, this is what hurt me the most, I am all torn."

Her story makes all of us join in her crying as an old man stands up telling her, "Believe me, all of them are going to hell. All of us are going to heaven…your husband, your kids, everybody who died here in the camps."

The older women pull her to the side, the same old man raises his voice, "God is bigger and stronger than the Israelis, one day

God is going to punish them a lot worse than they've punished us. So let's keep our faith, it doesn't matter if they kill us all or rape all our women, it is all written in the Qu'ran: our day will come."

Still standing, he continues, "When that day comes, God is going to give us the power as he promised through his prophet Mohammad as well as through the Qu'ran. He is going to give us the power to defeat them."

Not done with his speech, he yells, "They might kill most of us, but that is not going to kill our spirit. So if God wants us dead, then let it be; we cannot stand against God's will. Soon the whole world is going to find out what the Israelis did to us, to us who are unarmed and defenseless civilians! The whole world is going to see the truth! They only killed the women and the children and the elderly men. I am just curious what the Israelis are going to tell the world. How they are going to cover this massacre!"

Pointing his finger at Shatila, he shouts, "This is too big for them to hide! Our blood is not going to be hidden for long! Our blood is not going to be hidden for long!"

Now finished, the old man takes his seat on the red sand of the field. I am cheered a little by the speech. It is a moment of wisdom; everyone is hushed at its conclusion.

We sit now with nothing to do. From time to time I look back at the same woman. I can't help but think of her courage, how she watched her husband and children being chopped to pieces in front of her eyes; on top of this, to be raped in such vulgar fashion. She must be a true hero, to be standing after all this. Just when I was thinking that it could not get any worse, I see a woman like this. Yes, it can get worse.

The children's screams cannot be suppressed any longer, they are really suffering, probably not having had anything to eat or drink in two days. With the high pitched cries going on, a younger woman in the group begins untying a black sheet next to her that doubles as a knapsack. Her baby of about two months is wrapped in a blue blanket and rests in her lap as she rummages through the sheet.

Pulling a small plastic bag of greenish pita bread out, she calls the crying children to her, tearing the good parts of the bread into small portions. Turning to the side so as not to expose herself, she does the most beautiful and generous thing. Before passing out the pieces of the dry bread she milks her own breast to moisten it. I watch the children eat without complaint, they are happy to have something to eat. I am reminded of my own mother who used to do this for us when we were little, to see it again when I am eighteen is amazing and touches me deeply.

I know the bread is not enough to satisfy the children; I decide to go check the abandoned fruit and vegetable market that is located near the hospital, anything left behind would help. I tell the people I will be right back, running the short distance to the market. I enter the open empty building and search each stall. There is nothing salvageable, only rotten vegetables that are too-far gone and fruits that drip and squish in my hand. Refusing to return empty-handed, I walk swiftly next door to the hospital. I am unsure how long all of us will be stuck out in the field and it reminds me of the shelter days during the siege, before the massacre.

There are many dead people in the parking lot. They lay all the way up to the front doors of the hospital. I gingerly walk among them to the door. Inside I can see that the building is dark and bodies cover the floor. I am hesitant peering in at the doorway, unsure whether to enter or not. The scene is disturbing. It is too quiet, too dark. Blood still flows from some of the slain people. There may still be killers somewhere in the building. My mind debates until I see a man in a nursing uniform still alive, lifting his hand. My mind is made up, this place is not safe for food hunting and I back away slowly, staring at the still darkness. I turn and run back, without any provisions, to the field of sand where the group waits, sure that I have made a good decision despite my failure.

Once back, I feel the stares of the people wondering what I saw while I was gone. No one asks what I have been doing. I feel I cannot help these people. Sitting outside the circle looking at all of them, I feel out of place. There is no man my age among the group, I wonder what I am doing here if I can offer them no further aide. I am wasting my time. I should be trying to go back to the camp, trying to be there for Rola, the most important person in my life. I decide it is time to return to Shatila, even knowing for a fact that the odds are against me if I go back to that damned place. Not being able to see Rola these last two days has made me reckless and impatient.

Not wanting to leave without saying something, I explain as I stand, "I'm going back to the camp, I'm going to find out if the killing has stopped or not. This way we will know if we should wait here or go back."

The same old man who made the speech speaks up again, "Son, you don't look dumb or crazy, I strongly advise you to keep your ass here. Anyone in the camp would love to have your spot here. If you go back it is like you are asking to be killed."

He waits for my answer to this and wearing a serious face, I say, "I have to do this, I have to return to the camp. There are some people I truly care about that are still in there. I know they are still alive."

"If you are sure they are still alive then you should stay here. If you know they are dead then you should stay here."

No one can overcome the strong reasoning of this man with words. I tell him, "My decision is final, I am going back."

Still adamant, the old man replies, "If you go back you are dead."

"Didn't you just say not long ago that it is all written in the Qur'an?" is my counter.

He shoots back, "I sure did, and it *is* written, but you misunderstand that because God also said, 'Do not throw yourself into fire and say, it is written'."

He ends with, "I see, young man, that you have made up your mind. May God be with you—go ahead, go."

I turn on my heels, crunching sand underfoot as I walk back to Shatila. Taking safer narrow routes between houses, I stop before intersections, leaning against each corner and making sure the way is clear. I run across the larger roads until I feel I am getting too close to the main street where I can stand on higher ground so I scale a low building nearby. From the roof I scan the area for killers, my location is still too far to see. What I do see and hear are flies, billions of black flies thick in the air; they seem to have come from all over the world, have come following the trail of blood and thousands of dead bodies. They are too many to shoo away, I try to ignore them but they break my concentration by landing on my face and in the corners of my eyes.

I jump two roofs, now close enough to at least see into the street and I lean down not wanting to give myself away.

Raising my eyes, I spot a woman with hands tied behind her back being led by a rope in front of a killer; he walks her like a rich man would walk his leashed dog.

The terrified woman falls to her knees every ten or twelve feet, her feet barely able to carry her, she must know she is walking to her death. As she goes she walks unevenly, weaving through the piled bodies. The killer leading her walks in a straight path, irreverently treading on the dead. Each time the woman collapses the man pulls the rope, forcing her arms and her body back up.

Now the pair are very near, close enough for me to see the man's exasperated expression as the woman drops again to the street. The killer yanks the rope again obviously losing the last of his patience with the woman. I have no idea where the woman and killer are going. I imagine to her house, maybe she has offered him a ransom in jewelry or cash for her life. If this is the case I truly feel sorry for the woman. After eavesdropping on the killers the other night, I know that he will most likely murder her anyway after he gets what he is after.

I wait a minute or two after this pair passes by before jumping the two more roofs that separate me from the main street. Now I am not far from Rola's home, maybe four hundred feet is all. There is a nervous fluttering in my stomach, nothing can shake my hope though that she is alive and safe.

The gap is too big between the next building for me to jump. I look around, death surrounds me, the only life is the swarming flies who feed on the dead. My eyes peer over the shallow ledge of the

last building on the main street as I consider the final step of my mission. Once my feet hit the ground of the main street there is no turning back; I will be exposed and the next live person I face will most likely be one or many killers who will slaughter me on the spot.

None of this matters, the only thing I know is that I must reach Rola's house. I am on this roof for her and I was on a different roof witnessing the massacre for her. If it was not for wanting to reach her I could have escaped a hundred times over. I know Shatila better than anyone. It would have been easy to save my skin. She is the thing that holds me ever near danger.

Having already resolved to stand and drop down, my plans are aborted at the last second as I see a killer rounding the corner of a building in a side street directly ahead. Now flat on my stomach, I raise my eyes just enough to see that the killer is in a group of seven who are laughing and heading straight to the building I am laying on.

The group pauses in the main street, looking around at all the bodies; one man comments, "Wouldn't it have been easier if the Israeli army had dropped nukes on both these camps instead of us doing all this hard work?"

Another butcher answers, "Yeah, it would have been a lot easier, but do you really want them to die the easy way? We killed them in the worst ways available to human kind and still I am not satisfied. Look, we raped almost all the women here; not because we love sex so much, but because it is so enjoyable to rape the women of your enemies.

You do not know how much joy it gave me when I was slaughtering those little kids with my own knife. Do you know that every little pig that I slaughtered begged for their lives. This gave me the most joy in the world—to kill them while they still begged. Before I got here I didn't know that I had it in me to slaughter somebody. But I tell you what, the more I slaughter these people, the angrier I get."

The killer now spit on the pile of bodies next to him, three times raising his boot to smash into the face of a woman.

Another of the group speaks to the angry man, telling him, "Calm down Hitler, it's okay. We are all in this together, I witnessed everyone I killed beg for their lives too."

I cannot believe that these killers are making fun of their victims, it was not enough for them to slaughter the people in the most horrifying ways; these murderers are what people mean when they say cold-hearted killers.

The group of them still chat in the middle of the street, in the background through a house's open door I see three children, a man and a woman all dead and laying on the floor; the woman is hanging halfway out the entry way. There are men moving from side to side within the house stepping over the bodies. The sun glows orange as it sets, it is getting darker outside. More butchers come filtering in from all the side streets, I am amazed at their large number two or three-hundred maybe more.

Three killers emerge from the house I have been watching. The building I lay on is higher than the ones farther away across the street. I see killers coming out of so many houses, this is where I think they all must have hidden before the massacre's second wave.

I am relieved not to have jumped into this gathering of butchers. There is no way I would not have been spotted and captured. Once again fate has kept death from me.

There is a reason why all the killers are here at once; I do not know why but soon I will. To my left there comes none other than the same high ranking killer that laughed with the Israeli officer in front of the Jeep yesterday. He gave a speech then before killing the group of civilians. Now he plans to give another; in a loud voice he orders the butchers to gather close. His men obey, gathering close to the head butcher in charge, many stepping on the piles of bodies for a better view.

His face is very serious as the speech begins. "First, I want you to know that we went overboard in these camps. It looks like we were not supposed to kill that many people."

Disgruntled murmurings come from the group of killers at these words. The head butcher calls for silence with his hands, pressing the side conversations down, waiting for silence before he continues. "I know, I know, I agree with you. I don't think we went overboard here. I think we have done the right thing. But they say we went crazy. They say we killed women and we killed children. I guess this is supposed to be prohibited.

My superiors are taking heat as I speak to you, but we have our revenge for all the years we have suffered at their hands. I personally think that they got less than they deserve, if it was up to us, we would like to kill them all. Tomorrow morning the camps are going to be open to visitors and reporters from all over the world.

We have to make sure that those reporters are not going to see women and children dead on the streets. From this moment until the early morning hours we have to make sure that every dead child and woman in the camp has disappeared. The fun time is over, now is the real work. I promise you, if there are dead women and children in the streets come morning, then *we* are to blame. Not the Israelis, not the Americans. *We* are to blame. My superiors gave me a direct order to put these two camps in order before we leave. I want to make sure that my orders are followed without any objection. I do not want to have to warn you again how serious the situation is."

One of the butchers in the middle of the group raises up on his toes, shouting, "How are we going to hide all those dead bodies? There are thousands of them!"

Still serious, the head killer motions for this man to come forward, the others make way for him. When the man is close, the head killer seizes his hair, pushing the man's head to the ground. The ivory-handled sidearm I noticed on the head butcher now serves as a bludgeon. Three times he strikes the questioning man's head until blood flows.

The beaten man is thrown to the side, the head butcher lets everyone take a good look before saying, "I said the situation is serious, I said no objections. This is not a democracy."

The crowd of butchers are very quiet as their leader paces deliberately in front of them. He waits for the gravity of his order to sink in.

"From this moment on there is no cigarette break. There is no coffee break. There is no tea break. There is no break period."

Demonstrating with both hands and speaking slowly, he instructs, "I want every woman and every child in a pile here to my right. Pick them up from the houses, from the side streets, from everywhere. Gentlemen, this is a clean up operation. Some of you do not know what that means. I understand that, I don't expect you to understand it either. Just follow the order."

The head butcher claps his hands, motioning for his men to scatter. The scene is alive all at once, the killers running in all directions. A few stay in the main street, cherry picking the women and children from the existing piles. The dead are dragged by their arms and legs to begin the new pile demanded by their leader.

The head butcher continues to pace as he supervises the affair, somber and steady in his steps. The contrast between this speech and the boastful levity of his last, impress on me the amount of pressure that his superiors have imparted to him.

There are very few hours left for the extent of their crime to be hidden from the world. I am truly stuck on this rooftop, the leader of the butchers still paces, the killers swarm all around. Any movement from me will be easily spotted even in the growing darkness. While the butchers are busy I hear the rumble of a large engine approaching from the South. Far away I see the source of the noise, the large truck that I have seen usually pulling a trailer of tanks now parks with a different cargo—a big Israeli bulldozer.

Within minutes the bulldozer's engine starts up, this one louder than the last. It rolls down the trailer ramp, heading towards me, flattening bodies as it comes. The operator cuts the engine a short distance from the supervising killer. He climbs down and the two speak briefly with each other. The head butcher speaks fairly fluent English to the man, pointing the operator's attention to the south side. I see that the two are not in agreement. There is some misunderstanding.

The butcher tells the man, "Follow me," as he walks south, passing the bulldozer. The operator climbs back into his vehicle, backing up the machine to follow the head butcher.

When the bulldozer stops after about a thousand feet, I see the scoop digging, small mountains of brown dirt being piled to the side of what can only be a mass grave for the women and children. I understand now what the head butcher meant by "clean up" operation. Two killers at a time swing a body from one arm and leg onto the growing pile. In about an hour and a half there are three mounds of dead women and children piled as high as a man; by this time the bulldozer, judging from the large amount of dirt thrown at its side, has dug a sizeable pit.

The bulldozer backs up past the piled bodies and lowers its fork under the nearest one. The operator forcefully scoops a third of the bodies. The killers facilitate him by throwing more on top. Rolling heavily back to the hole farther south, the bodies are dumped, the bulldozer returns for another load; the process is repeated until someone has realized that one machine will not finish the job in time. Another bulldozer joins the first, digging the pit larger while the original continues its trips back and forth. Meanwhile the soldiers continue bringing the victims, the supply is bottomless.

The flares begin again, the Israeli army generously providing enough light for the killers to spot the specific bodies they need. The flares bring to the clean-up operation more than they bargained for as handfuls of survivors routed out of houses are pushed out into the main street. The killers have taken their orders seriously, there is no playing around; the people are shot quickly in the back of the head, execution-style. After four or five hours I see now that the butchers are tiring physically of their back-breaking job.

Two men carrying a heavy-set woman come from the narrow street across the way, not making it quite to the spot before

dropping her hard on the asphalt. Both killers arch their backs, stretching from soreness. In a few minutes they pick the woman back up, depositing her on the small pile of twenty or so other corpses. Slowly they make their way to the curb joining the many other tired killers on break who line the street.

The bulldozer operator returning from the mass grave, cuts the engine when he sees so few bodies are ready to carry. The operator climbs out of the cab, screaming in a thick Arabic accent, "What are you doing sitting on your asses?! I was told you guys you were going to work around the clock. That means no break!" Looking around and waving his hands, he asks, "Is anyone in charge here to talk to? This is unacceptable!"

One of the resting butchers stands to speak with the operator. He says, "Man don't just look on the main street, go look in the houses behind, inside the houses, in the small roads; there are thousands of them, they are everywhere! What we are doing is useless, even if we work all night long we are not going to be able to hide even ten percent of them."

The bulldozer operator loses his temper, saying, "It's a lot easier to kill them, but it's a lot harder to bury them; is that what you guys are telling me? Yes, we are not going to be able to bury ten percent of them if you are sitting on your asses! Okay, I'm going to make it easy on your lazy asses," he continues as he climbs back into the cab. The machine responds to the angry man with a thick black cloud of smoke, jerking as it moves to the nearest house. The scoop slams into the wall, demolishing the structure. The operator moves on down the street, crushing and shoving each house to the side. I assume he is razing the area so that the killers will have a direct path to get more bodies to the main street. As the walls come down I can see that the rubble is mixed with dead people, limbs, heads, cement, all turned and shoved together.

As the bulldozer demolishes, three killers burst out of that house's door, yelling at the man, "Are you crazy? Are you trying to kill us or what?!"

The operator pays them no mind, continuing to tear the house down. This man, a regular soldier, takes his orders more seriously than the Phalangists militia men.

Having stripped the houses down from the opposite side of the street the determined operator now moves to my side. One house then another, then the house under me starts to shake. The scoop has hit the far corner, tilting the whole surface under me to the right. The front wall is down, I do not have much time. The operator's face is hidden by the scoop but the killers in the street would see me if I stood. There is a door flush with the roof behind me that leads down into the house, I army crawl to the opening, sliding head first down the steps. Now inside the house. I have only seconds; I am between the living room and a bedroom.

I run to the bedroom and pull an old foot and a half thick pink spring mattress off the bed and completely on top of me, on top of my back. The house comes down all around me, cement chunks hitting the mattress and the floor all around. I can barely breathe from the pressure. The wall next to the bed is hit, it falls halfway on top of the mattress, rebar holds some of the weight. This is the end for me. After everything, this is it. My life flashes before me, I have taken too much risk with my life since the beginning of the

massacre. I have no reason to believe that I will survive this, and whisper, "Please forgive me Rola."

Fine grey dust thickens the air and through the narrow gap I see the tracks of the bulldozer grinding over the pavement as one track turns the machine away, smashing the front end of the mattress as it goes. The killers stare straight towards me, framed in the hollow tracks of the bulldozer. This is the first time I have been on the same level of the main street since the beginning of the killing, before I have always been above on higher ground.

The living room is exposed to the street, the mattress and the lump I make in it visible as well. The bulldozer moves on, heading for the next house, suddenly a screaming woman clutching two small children runs from this house, giving up her hiding place in order not to be buried alive. The poor thing runs past the roaring bulldozer, freezing in front of the line of killers. The machine carries on with its work, I wonder why the killers do not get up or move to capture the woman; they sit mutely watching her distress. Perhaps they do not want to add to the number of bodies to carry.

For some reason the operator shuts his machine down, staying in the cab a ways down the street. I watch the woman carefully, giving her my undivided attention; it could be me facing the killers next if someone shifts my mattress.

One killer finally breaks the silence, calmly asking, "Where were you hiding?" as if he were merely curious. Probably they were in that house before.

She answers from a terrified face, "We have a little shelter in the kitchen."

Another butcher adjacent to the first comments, "You don't have a Palestinian accent."

"Well, I am full blooded Lebanese," she explains. "There are a number of Lebanese living in the camps."

The killer who asked about her accent is not pleased with her answer, asking, "How about those kids. Are they Palestinian or Lebanese?"

She quickly replies, "Oh, they are a hundred percent Lebanese, their father is Lebanese too."

The killer rises, walks straight to the woman and says, "I swear by the Virgin Mary that if you *were* Palestinian I would not have hurt you or your kids. Because you are Lebanese, living among those pigs, that makes you worse than them."

"Well, we had no place to go, no home, no money. These Palestinians helped us, took us in. You cannot blame us!"

"You figure it wrong, I would rather die of hunger, die of thirst sleep in a trash dumpster before living with those pigs."

The woman steps backwards, her hands shaking from fear or from the weight of the children. She has lost the conversation. She may have lost her life.

The killer tells the fellow next to him to signal the bulldozer to back up towards them, the engine comes to life, chain tracks begin rolling. The killer snatches the older baby, a boy maybe four years old and throws him under the tracks. Blood sprays everywhere, the boy is smashed flat to the ground. The mother is hysterically screaming but not making sense. She is jumping in agony while still holding close to her chest the only baby left to her.

The operator cannot see what is going on, he follows the hand signals of the other killer in front. The woman crouches down when the killer comes for her younger child, shielding it with her

knees. The butcher yanks the baby free by its hair and throws it under the tracks as well.

The bulldozer stops and turns off, the operator climbs out on the small side ladder, suspicious of what is happening. He may have heard the woman's screams. I can see clearly in the reddish glow of the flares that hang five or six hundred-feet in the air, the atmosphere like a sunset. The operator jumps down off the steps, suspecting foul play as he heads to the rear of his machine. He passes the stain of the first baby, the flares reflecting in the spilled blood. The second child is just at the end of the tracks, also completely smashed, both blood pools seem to glow in the dark.

I am surprised when the man erupts, screaming, "No, no, no!" striking his hands on his chest in the manner of a grieving woman. The man grabs both his cheeks, digging his nails in so hard he draws blood.

He cannot believe what he has unknowingly participated in, screaming, "You sons of bitches, you children-murderers-killing-bastards! I have nothing to do with your insane revenge!"

The man lunges for the perpetrating killer, the others gather protectively around him, holding the violent operator at bay.

Meanwhile the young mother, in her mid-twenties, is pulling out handfuls of her black hair. Her clenched fists flailing her thighs and screaming with all her might. Her heart is broken, bleeding along with her murdered children.

The Israeli operator yells for the killers to get off of him, pulling the distraught woman up by her right hand to hold her tight to his chest. The man grinds his teeth, stabbing his finger at the group of killers in a silent dare for them to stop him as he walks the woman away.

The Israeli man releases her in the side street next to me, telling her, "You are free to go. I promise no one will hurt you."

The woman runs back to the same killer who threw her children under the bulldozer, screaming, "Please kill me! I don't want to live!" while kneeling to kiss the man's boots, begging to die.

The man turns to his friends, saying sarcastically, "Do you believe this woman? She is begging me, kissing my shoes to kill her! For the last two days people have been begging me to let them go, to let them live. Now she is begging me to shoot her. I guess you can't please them all, huh."

The woman is persistent, changing tactics, screaming, "You bastard child killers! You killed my children but you don't want to kill me?!" The killers' comrades stand silently, all backing away from the gasping woman.

The bulldozer operator comes close to her, touching her back, saying, "Why don't you just leave? It is not your time to die."

The man climbs back up into his machine and starting it up he rolls forward, the way he came. The woman watches and tearing away to the bulldozer's front she throws herself under the moving tracks, finally getting her wish. The operator once again is oblivious to what is happening beneath his powerful machine. One of the killers spitefully runs to him, shouting up at him that he has just killed the woman.

He climbs out again, standing by the side of tracks where the woman has died, just standing and looking for several minutes. Pacing with his hands on hips, I can tell the man cannot believe what is happening to him tonight. He has been entrapped, wants nothing to do with any of this. He gets in the bulldozer, heading

south to tear down more houses. I am nervous for Rola, the machine is turning into her neighborhood.

The other bulldozer has been digging nonstop.

Bright headlights race near from this direction, running straight over the flattened dead. An Israeli Jeep stops in the middle of the street right in front of the seated butchers and four soldiers climb out. The officer who was seated in the front passenger seat jumps out screaming loudly in English, a language I understand from having studied if from the first grade on.

"Come on, Come on! We need to finish all this! Tonight, tonight!" He repeats the last word twice, making sure the filthy killers understand him. Not getting a sufficient response, the officer motions with his arms for the killers to move, still yelling.

No one listens. The man angrily speaks into his walkie talkie in Hebrew. He listens to the response, then begins talking again while pointing at the seated killers. The officer looks up at the sky expectantly as dozens of flares are shot off from the hill, lighting the night even brighter.

Passing the radio back to the driver, the Israeli officer directs his attention back to the butchers, saying, "Seems to me you had too much fun here. You guys were not supposed to have that much fun! Get off your asses and clean up the mess from all your fun!"

He is inferring that the Phalangists were not supposed to kill that many people, referring to the necessary drudgery of clean-up after a party.

At this the butchers stir themselves, slowly getting up, splitting in different directions. Like the first time, the women and children are thrown in piles by pairs of butchers. Now the killers work in earnest, realizing the lateness of the hour, the closing of their window to hide. With nothing to do but watch the butchers piling bodies, I think it will be a long night. There is nothing but death all around me, piles of death rising higher and higher; I am in Hell watching the devil working. I watch the killers, they look human to me. They are far from it, more animals than anything human.

I employ myself while waiting by thinking, how the killers could bring themselves to kill women and children, surely they have wives, mothers, sisters and children. I wonder if they were raised to be murderers and butchers or were they trained up to it. Their work is professional quality, it seems like they have experience. Even after witnessing the massacre with my own eyes, my mind rejects that humans are capable of this atrocity against their own kind. There are too many questions on my mind, I doubt anyone can answer the breadth of them.

Watching the killers piling my own people in the middle of the street mentally exhausts me, this adds to my physical exhaustion. The pressure of the cement-weighted mattress hurts my back. I have not slept in a long time and despite the danger my eyelids are fighting to stay open. Falling asleep would be the worst thing because the killers are just feet away. I begin to notice that some of the butchers' routine has changed. Now I see some are carrying mattresses from the houses, even from houses further away, throwing them over bodies in the main street. I am not sure what they are doing it but I am obviously concerned about the safety of my hiding place under this mattress.

Two killers stand very near where I lay with their backs to me, within five or six feet. The cement weighing the mattress down on

top of me is a flimsy safeguard; the men would only have to pull it up to expose me. The killer on the right takes a walkie talkie from his back pocket, pushing the button. His exact words are, "Hey, we are shoveling shit here. Nobody told us anything about clean up before we got here. Is this really our job?"

Releasing the button and listening to the reply through static, the man speaks again, "Why do we have to pick up and bury those pigs?" Replying to another static-filled answer, he says, "Okay, okay, we're going to try our best."

This said, he returns the radio to his pocket, yelling to the butchers around him, "There's no way around it! Keep working, there's not much time before daylight!"

What the man says now to the one next to him interests me, "Why does this bastard have to come here in the morning?"

It must be someone very important who is coming to spur on such a large-scale clean-up. Things become clearer now. It makes sense that the mess is being covered not only to hide the massacre, but also in preparation for the "bastard."

The morning is soon coming and if I live long enough it is a matter of time until I discover the "bastard's" identity. Relief floods over me; the men are not after my mattress.

Another fear grips me. My stomach is growling loudly, the men might hear because the only ambient noise in the otherwise silent night is the sizzling of the flares. I have not eaten in three days, not since the massacre started but despite my stomach's grumbling I am not hungry at all, the death all around me makes food the last thing on my mind. I am dead if they can hear, I cannot even move my arms to hold my offending midsection; any movement will give me away.

The killers light up cigarettes, watching the others work. No one is resting now. The only idle men are the two in front of me; they must be of higher rank to have a radio, to have direct communication with headquarters in East Beirut. These killers have been working nonstop ever since the orders of the Israeli officer who had more flares shot up.

The bulldozer is back. The hardworking butchers have piled a worthy amount of bodies enough to call for the machine's attention. The bulldozer makes a couple of trips back and forth.

I decide to give my mind and heart a break from watching the repeating scene and turn my attention inward to the growing urge to hold Rola in my arms. The morning is near. It will not be long before I see her but, this time I will never let her go for any reason. Leaving Rola temporarily to go to my house was the biggest mistake of my life. If I had stayed with her in the first place we would have been together through all of this. I have learned my lesson the hard way.

I keep my eyes on the piles trying to approximate how many women and children are being buried; I have done this all along. I am not sure why I have bothered but something in me knows that I am watching and witnessing history and maybe one day I will tell the story to my own children…if I survive this to have children. Whatever the reason, I estimate that the number of women and children buried so far is between six and eight hundred.

The killer with the radio takes a long last drag of his cigarette then turns left to flick the glowing butt away. From the direction he turned it can only have landed on my mattress. The soft material of my heavy covering has the potential of turning my

hiding place into an inferno. I face a death-death situation. I have the sum of all I have been through during the massacre on one hand, on the other hand the possibility of burning with this mattress. I am forced to make a decision if it comes down to it...burn alive or run to face the butcher's axes in the street. The way I see it, these are my only options. I worry about the cigarette for an hour, but by now I would know if the mattress was going to ignite. My fears are relieved as I realize that if it was going to burn it would have already begun.

The cold-hearted killers work in the early dawn, the light is enough to cause the Israelis on the hill to cease firing the flares.

CHAPTER SEVEN

The World is Shocked

Saturday, September 18th

In the dawning light I see two army trailers pulling into the south side of the camp, the two bulldozers are hurriedly loaded. Minutes after the trailers pull out, lines of Israeli military vehicles filter into the streets. The jeeps and trucks are parked everywhere, even on the sidewalks.

Hundreds of Israeli soldiers flood into the street, yelling at the killers, "You have to leave immediately! You have to leave at once!"

Israeli officers and soldiers push the killers against the walls, pointing their fingers at them while shouting in English, "We said you have to leave RIGHT NOW! We are serious about this! Your time is up, we mean it!"

Butchers run from every direction like rats to the south end of the camp jumping into the backs of ready trucks that speed away.

Seeing the butchers leaving in a rush and the Israelis taking over the main street. I know that whatever bastard they were talking about is about to parade in front of me. A few straggling killers maybe ten or twelve, argue with the Israelis that they need to leave their marks behind before going.

A large gym bag full of spray cans is unzipped. All the killers grab one or two, shaking the cans and on what is left of the walls the men gleefully tag phrases like, "George was here. Tony was here."

Meanwhile, a few continue to argue with the Israelis. The soldiers concede and walk toward their trucks giving the killers a moment to spray more marks on the walls. I see the pride and joy the killers take in the job they have done in the camps.

I watch as the last of the butchers exit the camp, leaving in their wake one of the worst massacres in human history. I am relieved that I will no longer have to see the joyful faces of the killer butchers who have wreaked havoc here the last three days and nights. My excitement is overshadowed by doubt of whether the Israeli army's appearance is better or worse. I do not know what is going on so I resolve to stay under my mattress until it is absolutely safe.

Most of the soldiers are doubled over, holding their stomachs while retching in the street. It seems the men are not shocked by the sight. They may have been warned by their superiors of what to expect, but it is evident they are not prepared to meet what the killers left behind.

The sun is up in strength and in the clear light I see that the bodies scattered everywhere are human balloons, swollen almost double from three days' exposure in the open. The change in temperature between night and day has expedited the decay process. The color of their skin has changed to brownish black. The air reeks horribly of rotten flesh and expired blood.

Some elderly people trickle in from the side streets, leaning down as they walk among the dead, flipping bodies, searching faces; I assume they look for family and friends. They are taking a chance, it is still unsure what the Israelis' purpose is. I hesitate but the growing number of emerging survivors on the main street gives me confidence. Still the tight ranks of armed Israelis unnerve me.

I wonder why the Israelis are here at all, why they do not kill the people, evades me. I wonder if they wait for more to show up so they can finish the job. I retain the right not to trust these men, I have every reason in the world not to trust them. My people welcomed the Israeli army into the camps when they came to take Sports City as their base. They trusted them enough to surrender all their weapons and the result of this was the massacre of thousands of elderly, women and children.

Nine or ten Israelis stand in a group in front of my mattress, standing by with fingers ready on the triggers of M-16s. There is no one to fight them. Maybe they are scared of the dead bodies or maybe they are preparing to shoot what is left of the civilians. I struggle again with my options; to give up my hiding place or face the unknown with the soldiers. The pressure of the mattress on my back and of the wall resting on it, has cut the circulation from my whole lower body. My legs are completely numb, I am unable to move them at all.

A few minutes pass and I notice younger people have joined the older ones in searching through the bodies. It is time to take

my chances with the rest, I am no different than them. Slowly, I push my hands out from under the mattress into the street, pushing myself halfway up. The group of soldiers, seeing the movement, begin yelling in alarm as they grab my arms to pull me from under the weight but stop when I scream in pain. Several run to the side of the supporting pole where the hanging cement is attached. They push the slab off, lifting the mattress away.

A couple of the soldiers try to help me stand, I scream in Arabic, "DON'T TOUCH ME!" for more than one reason. Our blood has not yet dried in the streets, I do not want their filthy collaborating hands touching me also the physical pain of my numb legs will not let me stand.

They are not listening to me, they may not be able to understand Arabic, they still insist on helping.

I scream in broken English, "LEAVE ME THE FUCK ALONE!"

One answers back, "We are just here trying to help you."

I raise my head at this, screaming again, "If you wanted to help you could have helped my people when they were being slaughtered. Your help right now is useless!"

The soldier's tone changes, he looks around at the bodies, saying, "We didn't know anything about people getting slaughtered here."

In the beginning I was rude, now I am mad. "Don't dishonor the blood of my people by saying you guys had nothing to do with this!"

He is adamant, saying, "We had nothing to do with it! We didn't even know about it!"

Either this man is playing dumb or he really did not know but I am sure his superiors knew. Not only knew but also planned for the massacre. I give the man some proof, wanting to feed him some truth.

"I've seen some of the Israeli soldiers watching the killings! What about the flares, what about the bulldozers!" The soldier is quiet at this, we both know that I have won this round and he motions with his hands for the other men to back off, adding something in Hebrew.

They fall away, still watching me from a distance. In peace I begin the struggle with my body, pushing my hands beside me to roll excruciatingly onto my back. I sit, rubbing my thighs and calves to induce some blood flow. There is no feeling, I cannot move my toes or any part of my lower body. I begin to panic, thinking that I may be paralyzed. Legs straight, I grab one calf at a time, lifting my legs alternately for the sake of bringing some movement to them.

Still no improvement, the soldier who argued with me earlier steps back, saying in English, "Let us examine you, you might be hurting yourself by the exercises you are doing." I ignore him, he did not understand me before; I continue lifting my legs.

He pushes harder, saying, "Listen, these people on the street are already dead. We cannot help them, nobody can do anything about it, but we can help you."

I give vent to my physical and mental frustration, yelling, "WHAT PART OF FUCK OFF DID YOU NOT UNDERSTAND?!"

From this moment the mans seems to understand that I really do not want their help. Walking away, he says, "Suit yourself."

Still seated, I push myself backward to the supporting cement pole, hoisting my body up using the metal rebar. Now upright, I immediately hug the foundation pole to steady myself and rock back and forth, swinging my legs a little to encourage circulation.

As I do this, I see the soldiers are pushing the people away with their weapons, shouting in Arabic, "You need to leave now, you can come back later, but now you have to leave this street!"

The people resist being forced away from their searching, cussing the soldiers who interrupt them. Eventually the Israelis succeed in their evacuation of this side of the street.

Some of them come near where I hang, one asks something of the soldier who tried to help me while pointing his finger in my direction. The man waves them off, probably explaining that I cannot walk yet. The soldiers move on to clear out the opposite side of the street.

Now some warmth has crept into my upper legs, I shift over to the metal bars, raising and lowering myself for a couple minutes. There is feeling in my feet, I let go and try to walk. It seems like I am taking my first steps, having to learn to walk all over again; the small halting steps I take are difficult. I shuffle like an eighty-year-old man who uses a walker, dragging my feet, to the main street. This is the first time since the beginning of the massacre that my feet have actually touched the ground of the main street. Both feet planted on the asphalt, freedom rushes through my veins.

While I stand, the same Israeli soldier, persists in his one-sided conversation, walks to my side to smile and say, "You made it to your feet, huh."

I ignore him. He continues, "I want you to know you are a stubborn bastard, people like you scare the living hell out of us." I feel he is speaking on the behalf of the Israeli populace. Now he unsnaps the water flask at his side, unscrewing the cap before offering it to me. I look at him, refraining to comment before shuffling a few more feet ahead.

The man will not give up, jumping in front of me, bottle still proffered, assuring, “It’s only water.”

I am too slow to go around him, having trouble even to walk steadily. He looks me straight in the eyes, trying to put away any of my fears when he says, “It’s not poison, I swear,” before squirting some of the water into his own mouth to demonstrate.

I have to ask, “What, do you feel sorry for me?”

His answer is, “I don’t at all, on the contrary. I feel sorry for us.”

He brings the water close to my chest, saying, “Please.” Every cell in my body wants the water, I still hesitate to take it from his hand.

He says, “Believe me, you will still be my enemy, but I know you are in immediate need of this water.”

Finally I grab the water from him, unable to bring it from my lips until the last drop is gone. I hand the bottle back, saying, “Could you move out of my way now?”

Before he moves he asks, “One question, how long were you in that position under the mattress?”

I say, “I’m not sure, could be ten, thirteen, fifteen hours.” He steps to the side, watching as I drag my feet away.

Another soldier comes, yelling for me to get off the main street that they are sealing completely. The one with the water stops him, yelling a couple of words in Hebrew. The man backs off and I turn, slowly making my way to a side street that will take me to the center of camp.

The more distance I cover, the better I feel and when I reach my destination I am in good working order. There are hundreds and hundreds of people standing stagnant in the streets, trying but unable to get to the main streets to look for their family

members. Virtually all the people in the camp are related by blood or marriage. The Israelis have successfully blocked off the main street, preventing all from entering. I think they must be preparing for the arrival of the "bastard," the name that butcher gave him last night. As far as I can see, soldiers line both sides of the main street that runs the length of Sabra and Shatila.

Frustration is manifest on every face, all straining to see what is happening on the forbidden street. I can tell that most of these people have no idea what the soldiers are up to. I overhear conversations. Some say, "They must be trying to hide the bodies," others disagree,

"No, they cannot hide the bodies. There are thousands of them," another comments.

"Well, whatever it is, it's suspicious."

The anger of the people grows by the minute. An older gentleman yells out, "Let's march, all of us, to Sabra camp. From there we can try to enter through the main street."

Everyone, including myself, begins walking to Sabra, from Jalool land and passing Gaza Hospital, the crowd migrates toward Sabra. I am shocked and surprised to see a large number of reporters here who are also trying to enter the guarded street. The reporters are an eclectic mix, all shades of skin color and ethnicity; they all speak English with accents. I believe they have come, with their cameras, from all over the world.

The reporters are aggressive with the soldiers, pushing and fighting against them. The Israelis are aware of the clout these foreigners have from the countries that support them, unlike we, the Palestinians, who have no sovereign protector. If one of us were so bold there is no doubt that the offender would find his teeth or face busted by the bottom of an M-16. It has been proven that our blood is cheap, even free.

One of the Caucasian reporters, wearing a khaki shirt and vest loaded with film and camera equipment screams, “How many souls did you slaughter in these camps?!”

Of course there is no answer from the soldiers.

The same reporter, looking angry as hell, yells directly in one of their faces, “I’m talking to you, you murderers! How many souls did you slaughter here?! We are going in, we promise you! We are going in and we are going to tell the whole world about this massacre!”

The man does not stop here, raising his camera to snap photos of the soldier’s faces. The armed men restrain themselves from reacting to the provocation, knowing full well this reporter has immunity. My own patience is running out. I am dying to find Rola. The tension is broken by the sound of an Israeli chopper beating the air as it flies over some indefinite place to land in the camp.

The reporters shout with one voice, “What is going on inside the camp?! Is there a VIP coming to visit?!”

Of course the soldiers offer no answer. A few minutes later, one reporter from the front lines screams, “Is that Sharon?!”

At this question the reporters erupt into chaos; pushing, yelling, trying to breach the retaining wall of soldiers. The line cannot hold under this pressure and a few reporters break through before the gap closes. A couple of Israelis run after trying to capture them.

Another reporter yells loudly, “Indeed, this is Sharon!” as he raises his camera high above the soldiers’ shoulders, trying to get pictures of the Israeli Minister of Defense.

It is crystal clear now that Sharon is the bastard I heard the butcher speaking of. Standing on tip-toes, I see a tight circle of high ranking Israeli officers a few hundred feet off walking slowly towards Shatila in the broad street. I assume Sharon is at the center of the touring group of officers.

One old woman in front of me in the crowd screams at the top of her lungs in hopes that Sharon will hear, "I hope you are taking pride and joy in your work!"

Judging from the distance, I assume there is no way the group cannot hear her.

She continues, "Watch good, step in the blood, satisfy your hunger, satisfy your thirst! Enjoy the show! I know you are the director of this scene! May God burn you in Hell for eternity for this!"

While she screams, two soldiers with raised weapons make their way to the woman; a group of eight or ten reporters run to shield the woman from the imminent blows.

They face the two men boldly, shouting, "Murderers, killers, cowards! Murderers, killers, cowards!"

A woman reporter starts screaming, "Baby killers! Baby killers! Baby killers!" over and over for a whole minute; I estimate the woman hails from Germany.

When she stops, she fires off a loud question, "Why did you slaughter those people Mister Sharon?!"

The group was far, walking farther south; I am not sure they can hear. She repeats again, "Mister Sharon, why did you slaughter these women and children?!" After a pause, she shoots off a statement, "This is a war crime against civilians!"

Another reporter next to the shouting woman adds, "Don't call him Sharon, call him Mister Dracula!" The correcting reporter continues, "You have been thirsty for blood since you entered Lebanon, this time you got more blood than you bargained for. I hope you were that thirsty!"

The reporters' screaming goes on for the next half hour at least. The VIP must have left because the soldiers begin to back off, retreating before the now thousand-strong angry throng in front of them. The looks on the soldiers' faces are less than confident. They could not hold all of the people back now if they wanted to.

Most of the reporters who now face the scene are throwing up worse than the Israeli soldiers had. Many sit next to the bodies on the sidewalk, men and women both wailing and crying—nothing could have prepared them for this. What they see now has exceeded their wildest expectations. White face masks appear on the foreigner's faces, moved aside only to expel more vomit. The stench is too much for unseasoned senses.

As I walk among the dead and the reporters, one woman reporter passes a mask to another and I overhear her say, "Put this on, you don't want to catch a disease. You don't want to catch Malaria."

CHAPTER EIGHT

Free at Last to Find Rola

The way is finally clear for me to get to Rola. I find myself walking automatically to her house. All the time during the massacre I was sure I would run the whole way if I had the chance. Walking, for the very first time in my life I am scared to death. I am scared of what I will find in her house, even though I have kept my hopes up. The hope kept me alive. I have survived the whole massacre for the sake of this moment.

The closer I come, the heavier my feet get. My heart races, the pounding of my heart is actually audible. Buried deep under the fear, there is still excitement rising from the thought of seeing my girl again. I trip over the bodies as I go, my mind is shutting down from the fear; I am near blacking-out. At the end of this struggle I find myself on the front steps of her house.

The door is closed shut. Looking at the door, I cannot summon any power to push it open. I wonder where all the hopes I have tenaciously held on to have gone. I am drained by the thought of what I will find behind this door.

Heavy drops fall on my shirt, unbidden and unhindered by sobs, tears flow freely in a way I have never before experienced. I have no will to enter, instead I throw my head back, screaming her name, "ROLA! ROLA! ROLA!" without end. I desperately hope to see her coming out to me, saving me from having to come in to find what I will. Nothing happens. I slowly turn the knob, opening the door less than a foot to scream for her again. Silence, there is only silence in the house.

I open the door completely and step inside, a horrible stench greets me. The first thing I see is her mother in the corner of the living room. Silver duct tape is wound around her mouth, feet, and hands. She sits in a pool of dark brown blood, her blue robe soaked. Her throat is slit open to the spine, head back, resting in the corner with eyes open wide.

I drop to my knees, forehead to the rug in the middle of the room, screaming and crying. I pound the floor with my right hand, banging my head, not knowing what I scream. For a few minutes I cannot raise my head, my stomach churns. I spew out the water I drank not long ago, it is clear, having no food to mix with. Still crying, I crawl on my knees towards her, my feet unable to hold me. I trip on the roll of duct tape the killers have left behind. My knees are soaked in blood when I get to Rola's mother, I look in her eyes…she looks back. Her loss is as great to me as if my own biological mother had died.

I bring her head forward to kiss her forehead, screaming, "Sorry! Sorry! Sorry I was not there for you!" I pass my hands over her face to close her eyes, they open again, unlike what I have seen in the black and white American movies I watched growing up.

I twist to pick up the roll of duct tape, sealing her eyes shut with two passes. My six clicks knife serves to cut the tape. Before searching further I stand, walking in a daze back to the front steps outside. I watch the people going through the bodies, reporters taking pictures, women wailing.

I am in my own world with one thing going through my mind, *What if I had not left them before the massacre, what if I had stayed with them? What if I could go back in time, before the massacre? I definitely would not have left, I would have chosen to stay in the house and die with her mother.*

So many questions, so many what-if questions. Finally I realize there is no way around what I have to face, I might as well do it now. I have a feeling I know what I will find. I return inside the house, there is not a large space to search, only the single bedroom. I walk straight back to the remaining room, parting the blue ringed curtain in the doorway. Rola lays totally naked, half-draped over her bed with both knees spread on the floor, arms open wide on the bed spread.

I cover my eyes right away with both hands, here I am finally with her, alone in the bedroom. This is not what I had in mind, she and I at one time were going to be alone in a bedroom as husband and wife. She is the pride of the Middle East, she is the mermaid of the ocean, she is to me even more than this, she is the sun of the universe. She is everything beautiful. She is to me God's best creation. She is my soul mate.

I kneel next to her, stroking her beautiful black hair from around her face. As I do, I see something that looks like plastic tubes, slimy translucent white, sticking out from both sides of her stomach against the bed. I move a little away, rolling her from her stomach to her back, as I do long lengths of intestines tumble out from her, some landing on the bed, some on the floor. Blood is everywhere, trailing from the bed to the corner.

Now facing me, I see that her neck is all black, the bruising ringed with orange-blue. She has been strangled by two hands from behind; fingerprints are still visible, imprinted in blue. Both her eyes are totally black from being punched in the face many times, all her front teeth are missing from her mouth. I am compelled to examine Rola, I have to know exactly how she died.

I move the intestines aside to see that she is split open from navel to vagina. This does not make sense to me, the cut is perfectly straight and symmetrical. I fold her flesh back to where it should be, discovering that she had to have been sliced open from the inside. They stuck a knife in her vagina, pulling and slicing up to her belly button. I do not know why I am examining her, this is torture, fuel on the fire.

Something inside me wants to know the truth of what really happened to the most gorgeous woman my eyes had ever seen, the one who has captured my heart and my soul. At this moment my feelings are numb; I do not feel. I do not feel anything, I am still functioning through shock. I do not know if I will ever snap out of this shock or be able to live normally ever again.

I roll her back on her tummy, seeing clearly that she has been sodomized over and over again; she is wide open from behind.

Once again it is clear to me that the bruises on the neck, the broken teeth, the black eyes all point to her fierce resistance. Even so, the butchers had their way with her. Knowing Rola, they probably had to rape her when she was dead. I know down deep in my heart that she fought them until the last breath in her lungs; I truly believe this. If I think I know her as I believe I do, she would have given the butchers what they wanted only in exchange for her life and the life of her mother. Again, as beautiful as she is, she could have talked herself out of death if she wanted to. She chose death over living in shame; that's my girl. Another evidence of her fight is the manner in which the butchers tortured her body, revenge perhaps for the trouble she gave them.

Even in dying, she never let me down. This is why I call her a true hero. Now she is one of God's angels; if she is not, there is no furnace in God's kingdom. I have finished the examination, feeling better that I know how she died. I stand and walk to the living room to grab the duct tape roll. I return to Rola, filling the entrails back where they belong. I close the opening tightly, holding it shut with one hand, using my other to tear the tape with my teeth. I cut short pieces at first to close the flesh, freeing my hands to roll a thick band around her torso. She deserves the dignity and honor of having her body in one piece in death.

I walk to the kitchen, picking up a bucket three-quarters full of water and bring five hand towels from the bathroom. Rola's chest is crusted in black dry blood so thick it looks like rubber, she is not wearing a bra but it looks like she is. I set the bucket next to the bed, immersing three of the towels, throwing the other two on the small dresser nearby. Needing to snap out my shock for the job in front of me, I lean over the bucket, splashing my face a couple times. Bracing myself, I take two of the dripping towels, rubbing the thick blood from her breasts. I am aghast at what I discover next, more shocking than anything I have seen yet on her ravished body.

Both her nipples are missing, bitten off so deeply that the fat layer is exposed. There are teeth marks around where the nipples used to be. I stand from my kneeling position on the bed, jumping to the floor with hands shoved in my pockets, pacing in circles. I cannot believe I am facing all this alone. I am losing my mind, my hands cover my ears to block out the screaming I hear in my head. To have your nipples bitten off…probably while she still lived, the pain of it is unthinkable. I can only imagine what she felt as they were eating her nipples, can only imagine what kind of pain she faced. I cannot help but think of the butchers, of what kind of an abomination of human form they are? How could someone do that to Rola?

I feel I must find the nipples and tape them back, I lift her body to the floor. I remove the blanket from its four corners, taking it to spread outside the house under the sun. I hope the butcher spit them out; there is no telling, I go over every inch of the blanket, looking for the nipples. I find nothing after a thorough search. I toss the blanket aside, returning to the bedroom to look further. I leave no place unchecked, the far side of the wall, the floor, the mattress, the bed frame, even the pool of blood in the corner. There is nothing. It is clear to me that they have eaten her nipples. I find myself screaming, "WHY?!" They raped her, alive or dead; I do not understand why they had to do that to her body as well.

Knowing her so well, I know she would not give up her body to those mad animals even if they cut her flesh to ribbons. This is

what most likely happened. I take two six-inch pieces of tape to cover where her nipples used to be. I flip the mattress upside down and walk to the closet and take down a fresh clean blanket. I lay this on the bed and then begin digging in Rola's closet to find her fresh clothes. I lay these on the bed as well, then finish cleaning her body with towels and water. I imagine there is no blood left in her body to bleed. After bathing her, I carry her to the bed. I pull fresh pink panties on her and fasten a black bra. Then I put a black tee shirt and a long black skirt on her still body.

She is totally dressed, I put two fresh pillows on the blanket, moving Rola's head to rest on them. I take a comb from the bathroom and neatly comb her hair, still-wet from the bath. I stand now next to the bed looking down at her, in the clothes she looks like the Rola I know; only now her face is disfigured by the bruising and missing teeth.

For some reason I start a tirade of cussing everything and everybody. I blame the death of Rola on Yasser Arafat before blaming Sharon. I curse him for leaving the people of the camps without any protection. I stop for a moment to think—not understanding how he could justify leaving Beirut. Was he thinking our enemies would protect us? To me he is more responsible for this massacre than Sharon or the hands that physically killed her. I am mad at the whole world. Why did the girl I love more than anything have to be tortured, killed, and raped this way?

I am mad even at God as well, thinking that if he cannot protect the innocent helpless people then he is as responsible as Arafat and Sharon. When my cussing has relieved the pressure, I lay down on the bed next to her. I hold her innocent body in my arms, playing with her soft black hair.

I lay her head on my chest, even when life has passed from her for three days she still smells sweet, like fresh-cut roses.

The smell permeating the house is unbearable, it must be coming mostly from Rola's mother in the living room, mixing with the smell of the exposed bodies in the camp. I recline this way, not believing the extremeness of my broken heart as tears flow steadily in large drops to my chest soaking my shirt.

So many questions march through my head. It is awful for me seeing Rola already dead, it must have been doubly hard for her mother, if she had lived to see or hear the abuse of her only remaining child. I wonder if she had to witness the torture and rape before her throat was slit, or if they slaughtered her first.

For the last three days I have gotten to know the butchers methods. Knowing them well, I believe that her mother definitely was made to witness the horrific crime. This is how they found their fun, pleasure, and pride in their work. If I am right and this is the case, then this poor woman lost all her family members one by one before she herself was killed. She would not have desired life alone anyway. Like the young mother who lost her babies under the bulldozer, Rola's mother had the same kind of spirit.

This is a common situation in the camp. The killers did not just kill the thousands on the streets. My heart goes to the families who live, the ones who have to live with such horrible pain forever.

I am one of these—there is no life for me after this. The butchers killed me when they killed Rola.

My thoughts are interrupted by the sound of the door opening, by the time I jump up and get to the living room there are camera flashes. Two male reporters are standing in the middle of the room

taking pictures of Rola's mother. I shout at the fair-skinned, men in English, "What the fuck do you think you are doing?!"

One of them answers, "We are taking pictures, trying to cover the story in the camps."

I firmly tell them, "You are not taking pictures of the people in this house."

"Why? Don't you want the people of the world to know what happened to you people here in the camp?"

With tears dripping on the floor, I now shout, "I don't care about the people of the world! I don't give a shit what they think! They didn't care about us before, why would they care now? To them it is just going to be a story, something they read about."

One answers back, "You have the wrong idea about the people of the world, not all of them are like you think. We are here to educate them about your people, about what happened to you the last three days. We owe it to the thousands of dead people outside your door."

Aiming at Rola's mother, the reporter says, "If your mother were still alive she would want the people to know what happened to her."

He is not mistaken, she was a mother to me. I scream even louder, "When I want the people of the world to know what happened here, I will say it in my own words! One day I am going to write my own book about what happened to us, about what I have witnessed, about what I have heard—in my own words! Until then, you guys are not welcome here!"

One tries to reason with me by saying, "But until you write your own book, the people of the world want to know what happened today. They don't want to wait that long."

I escort the men to the main room of the house, shutting and locking the door from inside.

Next to the door, I pull my six clicks knife from my pocket and while turning back to them I say, "I don't want to do this, but if I have to, I will. Give me the film from the camera."

One of the horrified reporters says, "You are making a mistake," as they both back a few steps away.

I am not in the mood to argue and I scream, "THE FILM!"

At this, the one packing the equipment unslings a pouch from his side, unzips and dumps a pile of film canisters on the coffee table in the middle of the living room.

Irritated, I yell, "The film in the camera, every film you have taken!"

The one yells at his friend, "Give it to him, give it to him!"

He snaps open the back of the camera, placing the roll in my hand. I pull the length of the film out, exposing and destroying all of it.

One now says, "We understand your anger, we understand your pain."

Walking toward him, I bring the man back to Rola's bedroom, I ask, "You really understand? You guys got here *after* my people were slaughtered. I have been here since the beginning of the massacre. I witnessed the butchers slaughtering my people. I have witnessed everything, and I still don't understand. You just got here and now tell me *you* understand?"

He knows exactly what I mean. He walks around the bed to Rola as she lays on her side facing the wall. What escapes his lips is, "Oh my God! She is a gorgeous young lady."

Looking at me, he asks, "Is she your sister?"

I close the knife and return it to its place, saying, "She is my fiancé."

His eyes well up with tears, he and the other reporter who have entered the bedroom become quiet. The one who saw Rola first speaks for them both, "I want you to know we are very sorry for what happened to you here. We are sorry for coming into the house and breaking the moment with your fiancé."

The room is quiet again, my stomach's growling is the only voice willing to speak. The snarling sound is so loud that one of the men asks, "What is that, is that your stomach growling?"

I refrain from answering but the other reporter answers for me, "Yes, that was his stomach."

He asks, "How long has it been since you have had a meal?"

"About three days," is my unconcerned reply. The one with the equipment vest opens one side of it, pulling a Crunch candy bar from the inner pocket.

"Here," he says while extending it to me, "please take it."

I politely say, "No thank you."

"It will make you stronger, it will help you."

"You do not understand, if I eat it I will throw it up in a minute. My stomach is too upset to eat anything."

He replaces the bar in his pocket and I walk the two to the door, unlocking and releasing them to the outside. When they leave I look around, seeing many people mixed with the reporters going from house to house to see the extent of what the killers have done.

I shut the door, locking it again. I walk around the coffee table in circles for four or five minutes, trying to swallow what I am dealing with…I feel completely lost. I feel that I lost everything when I lost Rola. I do not know what to do from this point on. It is the end of the world, the pain in my heart is more than I can bear. Time has stopped. I drop to my knees, just screaming out the ferocity of my emotions with clenched fists raised.

Finally, I stand, walking to the bedroom to lay beside Rola once again. I talk to her as if she listens, telling her about everything I witnessed on the roof when I tried to get to her house. I tell her, in detail, everything I have seen. I tell her about the pregnant woman they hung by the hooks, how they stepped on the baby they tore from her stomach. I tell her about how they lined up the people, separating the men from the women and children to shoot all of them in cold blood. I tell her how they raped the little girl Nada, how they threw her off the roof after they finished abusing her little body. I tell her all this because I knew she was at home when all this happened, probably scared and hiding with her mother away from what was going on outside.

I want her to know that I was not hiding for fear of my life, that I hid in hopes of getting back to her. I could have escaped anytime, she needs to understand that I was in the middle of the massacre trying to survive only to return to her. I am late reaching her only because it was impossible to get to her. There were so many butchers in all the streets around her house. I feel I owe her this explanation, I do not want her to think I was hiding in my house waiting for the massacre to clear. After the whole journey and the risk of hiding in the carpet, in the shelter, under the mattress I feel it is unfair. I tell Rola, "I can't believe that you are the one who died and I survived, after I have been the one risking my life to get to you."

My explanation is followed by apologies, I say, "I am sorry, I am sorry," over and over, asking her forgiveness for not being there when I promised to protect both of them. I tell her, "I am sorry for letting them torture your innocent body the way they did for their own pleasure."

Her eyes are open, looking straight at me. I have no wish to close or tape them shut, I want to keep looking into them. I ask her to rest in peace, I apologize for being unable to revenge her death; probably no one can. I tell her, "I hope one day everybody involved in this massacre will face the same death that our people did from hands more powerful than theirs. I do not want them to suffer more or less death, just the same, in the same way we have faced. I hope this will happen in my lifetime, so that I can see justice served. Until then, justice is going to be blind."

While expressing these wishes and hopes to her, I clarify again that I am not wishing death to their families, just to the same people who planned and carried out this massacre. I am sure their families had nothing to do with this. Even through the pain I am still reasonable with my wishes for retribution. I am not wishing harm to the families of the Christian Lebanese Phalangists or to the Jews of the world, just the animals who killed my people. This is why I am trying in my wishing not to discriminate against Christian or Jew; I am sure not all Christians and not all Jews would agree with this massacre in any way.

Talking to Rola is an extension of my disbelief that she is dead. I feel I need some time alone to gain control of my mind and emotions.

I decide to go for a walk in the streets, to witness history. I could use the fresh air and exercise. Fresh air, actually, is impossible to find here because the stink of death rises from every corner and open space. I just need to be outdoors.

I take the house key from the end corner of the coffee table, locking the door now from outside; I want to ensure that no reporter or curious person will enter while I am away. Once on the street, I hear women screaming from every corner of the camp. They most likely have found what they've been searching for among the bodies.

I begin my journey, joining the others who wander in the streets, through the houses. We all want to read the book that the killers wrote with their own hands. The piles of bodies inside the houses, this is history, as morbid as it seems. Even though I have witnessed the massacre on the streets from my hiding spots, still I am unaware of what has happened behind the doors and walls.

The first house I enter is on the main street, I see seven bodies in the house, some sitting on the living room floor around a large aluminum dinner tray where the food is still untouched. In the middle of the tray rests the severed head of a little boy. I see the simple food consisting of boiled eggs, white cheese and brown beans on the plates. I look around the side of the tray and see a man in his fifties laying on his side with his arms tied behind him and his legs bound together with white ropes. His throat is slit in the same manner as Rola's mother. A boy of about fifteen rests next to the man, throat slit but unbound. Three children are on the left side, all under seven years of age. Two of them, a boy and girl, are slain in the same manner as the others. The remaining body of a little boy is missing its head. The head on the tray is his; this one received the abusive honor of a more creative death for some

reason. Only the butchers would know the answer to this question.

In the left corner of the room there is an upholstered sofa with red flowers and green leaves. On the top of this lays a girl, maybe sixteen, stripped naked with a slit neck. It looks like it was administered from a raping killer from behind judging from the sprayed line of thick dripping blood that contrasts with the creamy white wall behind the sofa. She is draped with arms and head over the back of the sofa, knees on the blood-soaked seat. The amount of blood from between her legs and her position is indicative of repeated rape.

What strikes me about this specific girl is that her clothes are folded neatly by the wall. Her black tennis shoes, blue jeans, red shirt and black panties all piled on top of a white bra: all of these items are stacked in a manner that no killer would have bothered with. I am led to believe from this and from the bindings of her father, that the girl was perhaps threatened with the lives of her family into undressing herself before the butchers had their way with her. Only then probably was the family finished off, after watching the rape and murder of their daughter and sister.

In the right hand corner lays another half-naked female, this woman is maybe twenty or twenty-two years old. She wears a black tee shirt and a black skirt is folded on top of red slippers sitting next to her. She lays on her right side facing the other girl on the sofa. I see she is pregnant, probably five or six months along. Her face is deep navy blue from strangling, the same white rope still tight around her neck. The ring finger on her right hand is cut off, it lays next to her. It seems to me that this particular finger probably wore a ring that the killers had difficulty removing. Her pregnancy probably causing the swelling that made it tight.

The last and seventh member of the family is a forty-something woman laying on the kitchen floor. She is dressed in a long black robe and white scarf, her throat is slit. Her right hand is severed at the wrist. The hand lays next to her and, like the pregnant woman, one of her fingers is missing—the left ring finger. I assume again that jewelry is the cause of the peculiar amputations.

I have seen enough in this house, I decide to go on to the next. Each house has a new story to offer from the dead within it.

Next door are three dead gray-haired elderly men that are spread in the middle of the living room. All three of them share one characteristic in common besides the gray hair, all of them were stabbed in the heart. The left side of their chests are dark with blood. I think from their positions on their backs that they must have been held down and stabbed.

On further examination of the house I find in a bedroom two naked women on top of a bed. One about eighteen, the other in her late thirties. I am sure from family portraits hung on the walls that the pair were mother and daughter. It looks like both suffered rape on the same bed simultaneously. The younger lady has a pool of blood between her legs, I can only guess she was a virgin. The mother's throat is cut open deeply, her head turned far left, unnaturally.

The daughter shared the same fate as the old men. From the expression on her bruised face, it seems like the raping killer tightly covered her screaming mouth before stabbing her through the heart. I cannot help but gape at the scene, thinking how sick the butchers are to rape the mother and daughter in the same bed at the same time.

I do not know if this is the result of sick fantasy or if the killers were too far beyond that lucidity. It seems they may have passed all reason. This type of thing is against all morality known to human kind. We are talking about mad animals here that could only have come from a jungle, no modern society would claim them.

I have seen the massacre from day one, virtually all females have been raped—no age was sacred. Old women, babies, and everything in between, all have been grossly violated. It seems to me the butchers are sexually deprived. This raises another fact: they did not come to the refugee camps only to seek their revenge, they came to satisfy their brutal sexual needs as well. A woman approaches me from behind as I still gaze at the two on the bed. She is upset, feeling the women deserve the dignity of not being on public display. She shoos me out of the bedroom, I understand completely.

Outside the bathroom stand two old men, frozen in shock. I move behind them to see what they are looking at in the small room. There is a young girl, about six, sitting on the floor next to the sink. She is dressed in a red knee-length dress. Her hair is tied back in a pony tail. Her small head now rests on her right shoulder and her feet are tied together in front. The butchers have played a sick game with her. The knot of the rope on her legs is tied in a simple shoe-string bow, it would have been easy for the girl to be free except for one thing—both her wrists are slit deeply to the bone. Her little hands lay on either side of her lap in separate pools of blood. The wounds could not have allowed her fingers or hands the movement necessary to untie the knot. She might have screamed or bothered the busy butchers as they raped her mother and sister, to deserve the clever torture of her slow death.

One of the men in front of me begins rubbing his hands in the motion of washing his hands of the scene before him. He cries, "What did this little innocent girl do to deserve this kind of death?" he raises this head, lifting his palms up to ask, "Where is God? Isn't he here watching this?"

Hearing the old man say this, he voices what I have been thinking all along.

The old man realizing what he has said, adds, "Forgive me God, forgive me God for doubting your power. You cannot blame me for doubting my faith when I am looking at this," aiming his finger at the little girl.

The other man is crying silently, he pulls a white handkerchief from his pocket and blows his nose. It is a shame for any man in this part of the world to cry, this scene on the other hand, calls for tears—there is no judgment.

I excuse myself past the men, entering the bathroom and untie the knot to free her legs before lifting her in my arms. I bring her to the bedroom, placing her next to the body of her mother and sister who are now covered by a black blanket.

The same old man who doubted his faith has followed me, passing a hand over the little girl's face to close her eyes.

He tells me, "This is out of respect for the dead."

I did not realize it was a matter of respect. I knew they should be closed but I was not sure why.

I am done with the history lesson in this house and begin to make my way through the people to the street. In the street I see a multitude of Red Cross ambulances picking up the dead bodies. The vehicles make me think of how much work they have in front

of them. The loads of two or three bodies per ambulance will not clear the thousands from the camp any time soon.

The workers wear paper masks and rubber gloves, the smell is too much for anyone to breath. The slimy bodies with flesh ripping away from the body is too grotesque to shield the workers by thin latex.

While standing in the bloody street, the same two older men exit from the house and ask me if I would accompany them to the next house. Out of respect for the older men, and out of my own fear of the unknown, I agreed to join them. As we walk by the three houses that were bulldozed the night before, I noticed pieces of body parts intertwined with the rubble. Here an arm, there a leg, I even saw a torso or two.

The fourth house down, amazingly enough, was left untouched. As I approach the house, I notice the unmistakable trail that was formed by the dragging of a dead body. I figured that it must have been made by a woman, since the butcher-killers had been dragging women and children out the night before.

I enter the house to access the damage and death and slowly approach the living room. There on the floor lay a man in his forties that was shot point blank in the forehead. His body is sprawled across the living room rug that has soaked up his cold blood. As I am kneeling over the body I am startled by a scream coming from the back of the house.

I jump out of my skin when the old man screams, "You have to come and see this."

I run to the kitchen to see the two old men standing next to the sink with their mouths gaping in horror. To the side of the sink I see a white washing machine with a front access door. My own eyes want to shut as I peer through the glass window to see two little girls. The smaller girl couldn't have been more then a year old and the older one probably was going on her third year of life. I saw half of each of the girl's pale blue faces. The poor girls must have suffocated since the only handle to the machine was on the outside. In shock I walk closer to the older men and in one sweeping motion all three of us take a closer look to make sure our eyes weren't playing tricks on us. We cannot believe what we are seeing.

As we straighten ourselves the older man who in the previous house had lost his faith, said, "Why does our blood have no value? How come we have no human rights? Who makes our children's blood so cheap or even free? Why are the children of the West considered the future of the world and ours are not?"

The other man responds, "The West considers our children future terrorists. That alone makes it okay to slaughter them while they are still babies."

The faithless man agrees and says, "If one single child in the modern countries is killed, the authorities would open an investigation and would not rest until someone is brought to justice to face the punishment of the crime. I hope this will be the case in these refuge camps. Hopefully, someone will care enough about these children to bring their killers to justice," he says as he points to the two little girls crammed into the washing machine.

"I only hope that some nations in the free world know that our blood and our flesh is equal to their own, especially when those counties believe that all men are created equal."

He continues on to say, "Only time will tell if they truly believe that or if they are just words without meaning. Only time

will tell if our blood will be lost forever or if somebody will take responsibility for this massacre."

As he starts feeling dizzy, he suggests we leave and the other older man and myself help give support to the unstable man. We take him outside and help him sit on the sidewalk to breath in "fresh" air.

While he sits on the sidewalk I need to stay close. His face is pale as can be and I want to be sure he will not need my assistance any longer. I notice a man walking towards us wearing all black, he starts to open his mouth to ask us if everything is okay as he wipes his own tears away with his handkerchief. I think the men know each other, but I don't know how.

The mysterious man in black says, "I just came from the Minded family house, I advise you three to not enter that home."

All of us knew the Minded family, the father was the owner of the auto repair shop in the Shatila camp, they are Lebanese. The man in black wipes more tears away as he says, "Those butchers, they slaughtered them all, women, children, thirty-five to forty family members. You cannot tell what limb belongs to what body, it's a mess in that house." And he left us there on the sidewalk picturing the Minded house in our imagination as he walked away.

The faithless man started to rise and he said, "I am going to have to go and see for myself."

"I don't advise you to," the other man said. "You're not in any shape to go there."

This is when I realize that these men had planned to visit each individual house. I have had enough, I can not continue showing my heart these awful scenes. I want to see up close what the bulldozers were doing the night before. I can see the Red Cross workers tossing bodies into the massive grave. As I approach the mass grave, I can see two rows of bodies neatly laid in a line. There is a machine that is spraying out a white powder as one of the Red Cross workers sweeps it over the bodies while another pumps the machine to create more power. This is a chemical that will keep the diseases encapsulated in the bodies, like a cast to a broken arm.

Once the bodies were dowsed in this powder, the bulldozer came to move them to their resting place in the mass grave. When all the bodies from that batch were placed in the grave, the bulldozer covered them with a thick layer of dirt. The Red Cross members did this to keep the smell to a minimum and contain any diseases that the decomposing bodies might carry.

I survey the area of the mass grave and notice a truck unloading large sized bags of white powder. I have a thought all of a sudden that I should help them. I walk to the truck and ask the man in charge if I could be of any service. He puts me and six other men to work to help unload these fifty-pound bags. I help unload the truck and when it is empty, another truck takes its place.

The whole process takes about an hour and a half. During this time I became comfortable talking with my coworkers and after we are done unloading the trucks, the man in charge asks me if I could stay and help bury some of the victims. These people are my family, friends, and neighbors. I can't deny my assistance to help the Red Cross workers bury my own people.

I am given the proper equipment for the job, such as a mask, gloves, and a vest that sports the Red Cross logo on its front and

back. After putting all the materials on, I start working. Fadi, my partner, who is Lebanese and about the same age as I, unload the next truck that arrives and place the bodies in rows. The other men spray the bodies down as we drink water to quench our thirst. Fadi and I talk about the massacre as we work. He is interested in knowing what has happened in the last three days. I share with him my experiences.

After working for three hours I become aware of the empty feeling in my stomach. It has been three days since I last ate and now feeling woozy and faint I decide that I feel comfortable enough to ask Fadi, "Would you do me a favor?"

Right away he says, "Sure," without any hesitation.

"Before I get totally exhausted, there are a couple more bodies that I need to bury, and they mean a great deal to me."

"Where are the bodies?" Fadi asks me.

"They're about five hundred feet or more in that direction," I say as I point my finger north.

"Let's go get them," Fadi says with commitment, and without asking me any details, whether they are men or womean, or how much they might weigh. He is up for any mission I feel I need to do.

Fadi and I walk side by side, he is still amazed that I have survived the massacre while at the center of all the blood shed. I can tell that Fadi is saddened by all the death that was brought upon this camp, and knowing that he volunteered for this job, just proves to me that he cares about innocent people and he's not even being paid.

I didn't even notice that we had arrived at Rola's house. I ask him for a moment alone as I walk up to her front door and pull the key out of my pocket to unlock the door.

"Excuse me for another moment," I say and walk into the house alone. Standing in the living room I see her mother and since she was to heavy for me to carry I begin gently dragging her by her hands to the front door where Fadi helps me take her outside to the street. I turn to lock the door behind me so that Fadi and I can carry Rola's mother to the middle of the street.

Fadi and I wait patiently for the truck that is assigned to this particular mission. Once it arrives, Fadi and I carry the body to the back of the truck and we carefully place her on top of all the other victims. Fadi and I walk next to the truck being careful not to step on the bodies that litter the street.

Fadi and I arrive at the mass grave, and we unload Rola's mom's body next to all the others. I ask Fadi for some time alone as I try to fight back the tears. I try to distract myself with work as I cover her body with the white powder, but the tears pour out of me. As I finish spraying her down, Fadi comes to my side. I grab her legs, and he her arms, and we lower her into the massive grave. It is hard for me to watch the dirt pour over her, but I continue watching until I can't see her any longer.

Fadi turns to look at me and asks in a sympathizing voice, "Is she your mom?"

I turn to look him in the eyes and say, "Yes she is my mother."

Fadi places his arm on my back and gives me a gentle pat, non-verbally saying he is sorry for my loss. I am staring at the mass grave when Fadi walks toward the man in charge and talks with him as I reminisce over what I have just done. I assume that Fadi has told him that I've just buried my mother and a moment later they both approach me, the foreman tells me to take a break.

"I'm fine. I can work," I say.

He replies, "I insist, besides when you come back, there will still be plenty of bodies to bury."

Since he is the Red Cross's man in charge, I feel this is the best opportunity to ask the question that was been weighing on my mind. I ask, "In your personal opinion, how many dead bodies are in both camps?"

"It's hard to know, but I can tell you roughly by the numbers I have seen, I would say between three and four thousand men, women and children," the foreman says.

"I watched the butchers last night bury six to eight hundred women and children," I say.

The foreman replies, "Yeah, we know all about that, we can tell since we are burying the rest of the people in the same spot they used."

"With those people buried last night, what will that take the number to?" I ask.

"For sure over thirty-five hundred people," the foreman replies.

With that said I decide to take my break. I turn to walk back to Rola's house exhausted physically and mentally.

Walking back towards Rola's house, I can not help but notice that on both sides of the main street, the number of bodies sprawled on the road, is decreasing; however, the sheer number of flies is increasing dramatically. The flies are feasting on the multiple numbers of decaying bodies. This makes it hard for me to reach my destination. Arriving at Rola's home, I grab the key that unlocks her front door.

Opening the door I see thousands of flies are hovering over the floor where the body of Rola's mom once laid. I quickly grab a pillow case that was folded in a pile of clothes on the couch. I use this as a fan to help me relocate the flies to the street. Fanning them outside is easy since it is still light out.

Walking in to the adjacent room, I see Rola's body covered in a blanket of flies. I use the same pillow case to remove the flies from her body and I quickly close the curtain between the bedroom and living room behind me, preventing the flies from returning to the bedroom. I keep swinging the pillow case to move the remainder of the flies out of the house and once all the flies are out of the house, I shut the door. I begin to look for the source of the flies and I stroll into the kitchen to find that a one foot by one and a half foot window is shattered. I grab the duct tape, which I had clenched in my hands, and use it to tape the pillow case over the open window.

In her bedroom I sit down in the chair next to Rola's bed. I can not help but to stare at the woman I love. Tears are falling down my cheeks as I tell her that I just buried her mom.

"She looks like she is finally at peace with herself and God. I am sure she is in heaven, as you are, but again you know that. I am sorry that I have not buried you yet, for my own selfish reasons I cannot let go, not yet. I promise you that I will bury you when I am ready. I am sure that if the roles were reversed, you would do the same in order to spend a few more moments with me."

I move slowly to sit beside her on the bed. I grab her body and pull her to me, resting her head on my chest. My hands instinctively run over her head as my fingers are intertwined with her hair.

"Do you remember the shelter days when you used to wait for my return outside with missiles falling from the sky? You

were willing to die for me. You are and will always be a true friend. I have never known anyone with such a strong will and personality. Since the day we met, we have gone through a lot together. You and I have helped a lot of people, we have shared the same suffering, and we have shared the same life. Except this time you suffered a horrifying death alone without me. I am here alive, feeling shameful because I wasn't with you when you died. I should have died with you. I made a promise to you that I would be there for you, to protect you. I feel that I broke that promise which has resulted in your death."

Tears are streaming down my face like water running off a cliff. I squeeze her harder when I choke out, "Will you forgive me, please?" My eyes are growing tired and heavy as I hold on to Rola.

Waking up a few hours later, I hadn't realized that I had fallen asleep. All I see is darkness in the room, but I feel Rola still resting on my chest. I move Rola from me to lay her flat on the bed.

I come to my feet and reach into my pocket for my cigarette lighter. I flick the lighter until I have a flame that I can use to locate a candle. I have no luck finding such an item. Walking out of the house I am surprised to see the men of the Red Cross still working without rest. I walk over to them and ask, "Does anyone have a candle?"

"Yeah, would you like one? We have been passing them out all day," the worker says as he walks to the front of the ambulance.

He opens the door, reaches into the back seat and grabs a plastic bag filled with about a dozen candles. "Would you like more then this?" he asks, and I reply, "Thank you, that's plenty."

I light a candle as I walk to Rola's room. I place six candles strategically all over the room to provide me with a sufficient amount of light. I glance at Rola lying on the bed and I can see the reflection of the candle lights in her eyes. I can't bare to close them, this is my last chance to ever gaze into her beautiful brown eyes.

I sit on the edge of the bed, my stomach growling, making me aware of my hunger, then I smile and say, "I know that if you were alive you would want to make me a sandwich right now, as usual." As these words pass my lips…I realize that she is dead.

The right side of her face that was resting on my chest is now visible to my eyes. I notice that the color of her right side has changed to black as gravity has allowed the blood to find a resting place. My heart feels bad as I come to the understanding that I have to bury her.

"I know you are looking forward to being buried." I say as I begin planning the next hour.

CHAPTER NINE

A Time to Bury

Without any hesitation I pick Rola's body up and cradle her in my arms. I walk through the living room in the dark towards her front door. I open the door with my right hand, clutching her tightly in my left arm. I walk out onto the main street and head towards the mass grave, her final resting place. My heart is bleeding on the inside for I cannot give Rola her own solitary grave.

Walking on the street, with Rola in my arms, Fadi sees me and runs towards me with a couple of the Red Cross volunteers.

"Let us give you a hand with her body," he says.

I say, "No, I am okay."

Fadi is becoming a little concerned, "I know you are weak, it is okay to let us help you."

I shake my head as I say, “It’s about honor, I want to carry her all the way to her grave. You do understand don’t you?” as tears fill my eyes.

Noticing how hard this is for me, Fadi simply says, “Sure, I understand.”

I think that Fadi feels the agonizing pain that I feel at this time and that he understands. Right then Fadi starts waving his hands to get the attention of an ambulance driver. I haven’t a clue why he does that, but I realize as the vehicle approaches me that Fadi has done that to shine light on the ground in front of me to prevent me from tripping over the dead.

The three men stay next to me as we walk at the same speed as the ambulance towards the mass grave. Her head lies limply over my shoulder and her arms swing gently as I walk. Half way to the destination I start to feel my arms shaking, and my knees about to give out. I stop momentarily to regain the strength I would need to take her all the way. I gently lay her body on the ground as I rest beside her.

A few minutes later I began to stand up when I am interrupted by one of the Red Cross men, “Let us help you with her body,” he says.

I scream at him, “No, keep away from me!” and I pick up her body to continue my journey. I know that these men are here with me, walking beside me, however, I have never felt so alone. This is the hardest thing I will ever do, all I want is Rola here with me to help me through this. With Rola by my side, we could accomplish anything. Unfortunately she is my mission and therefore the reason I am so heart broken.

I approach the mass grave with the last of my energy. I place her pure and innocent body on the dirt next to the grave.

I am having second thoughts about this being her final resting place. I sit down next to her in our final moments together, memorizing her face for the last time. I am not sure if I am ready to let go of her. I start thinking of the time we've spent together and how valuable that time was. In the distance I see the volunteers just tossing the dead into the mass grave, as if they were bags of trash.

Could this be it? Is this how her life is measured? I can't bare to leave her in this mass grave even though I know there is no other alternative. At this moment Fadi taps me on the back, breaking my train of thought.

"We can take it from here, you don't have to watch this," Fadi says with a look of sympathy.

Looking up at him with tears in my eyes, I say, "Again, it is a matter of honor. You have no idea what this girl meant to me. She alone is the reason why I am alive and she alone will keep me living."

The two men that had walked with me moments earlier down the street are now bringing a bag of white powder my way.

I immediately come to the thought that she should be buried naturally, so I inform the men that she will be buried without the powder covering her body. Again, they respect my wishes.

I ask Fadi for one last favor, "Just one more minute please," and he turns to walk away from me.

With the sands of the hour glass gone, I tell her, "I am going to miss you for as long as I live. You will always hold a special place in my heart, as well as in my mind." I hug her so tightly, knowing that this will be the last hug and contact that I will ever have with her. I kiss her head as I force myself to do what she would want me to do—to let go.

I wave for Fadi and he comes to help me. I am glad I have someone here to help. I tell Fadi, "I will jump into the grave, and I want you to gently pass Rola to me. I don't want her tossed into the grave, I want her to be placed in a gentle fashion," and Fadi nods.

I jump into the grave, numb to what I am doing. Fadi gently starts to move Rola toward the edge. He holds her firmly by the hands as I guide her down by her feet. Once Rola is in my arms again I hold her tightly, facing me, like a child hugging a life-size stuffed animal on Christmas morning. Our faces touch one last time, our noses slightly poke each other, my lips brush against hers, it is almost more then I could handle.

I need to place her in a spot where I feel she won't be forgotten. With no disrespect, I walk over the bodies that line the grave toward the farthest left hand corner. Here is where I shall lay her, here on the edge; few people would be buried on top of her in this section of the grave.

"Lay in peace now, your mom is buried in the same gave with you. You can be together forever. I know you will like that. I now know where you are buried and I can come visit you every day.

"What I am about to say breaks my heart because I never said it when you were alive. Rola, I love you with all my heart and I promise you I will never love another woman as long as I live. You are the only woman residing in my heart, and always will be. You have made me a better man just by allowing me to love you, and to be loved by you. You are the angel of love…my angel.

I'll see you in heaven, if I make it there. Please forgive me for not sharing this resting place with you." And I give her a final kiss.

My heart rips away from the wall in my chest as I began to lay her down. I straighten her clothes and make sure she is in a comfortable position. I start to stand when I feel my knees begin to buckle. I inhale a deep breath and force myself to climb out of the grave. I am sitting on the top of the hole watching her body slowly disappear as the brown dirt covers her body. With the last load of dirt, Rola is gone.

I thought I would feel worse, but I feel better knowing that Rola is buried with so many innocent people; men, women, and children, all finally at rest. Taking the last hour all in, I am grateful that Fadi has come to sit beside me. He offers me a cigarette, not knowing if I am a smoker but he senses that I might need to release some stress.

Lighting his own cigarette, he says, "You are an amazing man. You helped us unload bags of chemicals; you helped us bury a huge amount of bodies, without giving priority to the burying your own mother first. Only when you were exhausted did you bury your own mother."

With tears streaming down his dirt covered face Fadi says, "I can't imagine the pain you are feeling at this moment as I watch you bury this young gorgeous lady. I do not know if she is your sister or someone else, but I know that you have a great amount of love for her."

My mind is so numb that I don't care about the kind words Fadi has just said to me. I only want to focus on the spot where I had seen Rola for the last time.

It is hard for me to respond in a way that may not hurt Fadi but I can't handle sympathy at this time. I say to him, "Fadi, you are a great guy. You have been working nonstop to help bury my people and I respect you for that. I am sure that our paths will cross again some day, but now I have to go."

Fadi nods his head asking me, "Is there anything else I can do for you?"

I reply, "You have been doing a great job for everybody in the camps but, I will be just fine. Goodbye and thank you," as I walk away in a random direction.

I have a desire to be alone at this time, so I walk for quite awhile only to end up at Rola's house. I let myself into the now empty house and head towards her bedroom. Entering into the room I notice a pool of blood that had collected near the bed as the candle lights flicker devilishly in the reflection.

Not knowing what to do I open Rola's closet door. I picture her in different clothes as I glance through each item when I see her brown photo album. I reach to take it and begin skimming through the pages as I sit in her chair next to her bed.

There are so many pictures of her when she was five or six years old. I had never met her father and brothers before they died. I now feel by looking at these pictures that I am acquainted with them.

Finishing the album, I reach for the closest candle to light my way towards the kitchen. On the stove is a kettle with a lid. The aroma smells stale and as I take the lid off I think that just before the massacre took place Rola must have been cooking brown beans and cubes of meat. She must have been making dinner for me.

I sit the candle on the side of the stove to grab a spoon out of the utensil organizer and begin to eat straight from the kettle. The food tastes good but with a hint of sourness, the meat has obviously gone bad but I am so hungry I continue to eat for the thought that this was the last meal Rola will ever cook for me. I can't let it go to waste.

Knowing that the food is bad, what is the worst that could happen? Am I going to die from the food? Then this dish would be doing me a favor. To me it would be a perfect situation as I am not so big on life at this time. I eat the last bit of food from the kettle then I grab the candle and head back towards the bedroom. I return to the chair where I pick up the photo album flipping back through its pages until I fall asleep staring at her picture.

A knock on the door awakens me. I walk to the door and swing it open. The sunlight blinds me as I try to open my eyes feeling rejuvenated from my slumber. I realize an old man in his seventies holding a white cup is standing before me. He is dressed in black slacks, a brown shirt, and brown leather shoes and he has a friendly kind face.

"Oh, I am so sorry, I didn't know that you were asleep. I'll just come back later," he says as he turns to leave.

I quickly perk up and say, "It's okay, what do you need?"

He extends his hand and asks, "I just wanted to know if you could spare some sugar. I made some tea, but I found out that I have no sugar."

As I begin opening the door I reply back to him, "I am not sure if I do or not, but please come in, I'll look in the kitchen." I ask him to stay in the living room while I go search for the sugar.

In the kitchen among the row of jars I open a blue jar to find it is half full of sugar. I head back towards the living room with the jar and say, "I have no need for it. You may keep it," handing him the jar. He thanks me for it and he tells me that he lives next door to Rola's house as he turns to leave.

"Please wait!" I say with great anticipation. He stops to turn and face me. "Where were you during the massacre? Where you in the camp?" I say.

He replies, "Oh yes, where would an old man like myself go?"

I ask him another question with a curious look, "Were you at home?"

"Yes," he replies. He can tell that I have many questions just by looking at my face. "Do you want to know why I am still alive?"

Silent and waiting, I rethink my question so that it will not offend the old man.

The man continues without my response saying, "They came from the south, arriving at my house before coming here. We were in the living room, all of us about to have dinner. There was a knock on the door and my grandson went to open it. Six of the butchers entered our home and gathered all of us into the living room. They asked all of us to put any money and jewelry that we might have on the floor. My wife had some money tied in a handkerchief stuffed between her bosoms, she retrieved it and threw it on the floor. The man criticized that it wasn't much money, but that was all that we had to give him. I took off the antique watch that I had inherited from my grandfather and tossed it into the middle of the floor, giving them all the money and jewelry that we had.

One of the butchers became very angry and screamed, “Are you kidding me? Is that all you have?” I don’t think that they believed that this was all we had to offer. This is when three of the men grabbed one of my sons forcing him to the floor and cut his throat from ear to ear as a sign of warning. If we had money or jewelry this was the time to get it out. I personally swore in the name of God that I had nothing else to give. This said, the butchers began killing everyone including my other son, two daughters-in-law and four of my grandchildren—the youngest a two month old baby girl. She was bundled in a pink blanket when they disrobed her and with one of her precious legs in each of their tainted hands broke her open as if they we breaking a wish bone from a turkey.” Pausing to take a deep breath and regain his composure he fought back the tears welling up.

“My wife died of a heart attack while watching her family being slaughtered. We had been married for fifty-three years, I would have never imagined that I would lose her in this fashion, but again it is God’s will. I have to respect that. I lost my entire family in only five minutes. I have spent my entire life working hard just to provide for them and to watch my children give birth to their own. They were supposed to take care of me at this stage in my life.

“Now I am all alone, struggling to make myself a cup of tea. The answer to your question as to why I am still here is still unclear to me. All they told me is, “There is no need to kill you, you will die today or shortly after,” but that is where they are wrong. It is all left to God to decide when I leave this world. Who knows, I might live to be one hundred.

"When they were done with my house they went next door. hey came here. I tell you, I couldn't stay in my home with my family dead so I went outside to have a silent moment with God. I won't ever reveal to you what was said on my part. Is too private and painful," he says, while holding the jar of sugar.

"When I was outside I heard the screams of Rola and her mother. They were monstrous screams. I can tell that they were being tortured. I watched so many butchers entering this home, I believe at one time there was as many as eleven or twelve in the home.

My heart reached out for the young lady in the house, I could tell she was being raped repeatedly. I am not one hundred percent sure, I can only guess, but why else would she scream in that manner. After awhile the screams from the mother stopped, and only the screams of the daughter were left to fill the house. Maybe I shouldn't be talking about this anymore; it must be painful for you, as it is for me." He stopped talking and begins to walk away.

I grab him by the shoulders and beg him to continue on. "You are the only living person that can tell me what happened in this house during the massacre," I say emotionally.

"Sometime it is better for a story to go untold." The elderly man says.

"Not this one," I say with a look of horror in my eyes, "I really need to know."

He looks at me and sighs, "If it means that much to you then I shall go on. The solo screams continued on for almost an hour and a half. I'll tell you that this young lady was very brave. She gave those butchers a hell of a fight. I watched one man exit with blood running down his right arm. I could see that it was a nasty result

of teeth marks. Minutes later, I watched another butcher exit with his face bloody and scratched. She must have dug her nails in deep to cause that kind of damage." Smiling, he continues on, "Believe it or not I heard men screaming from inside the house. If it makes you feel any better, she wasn't an easy target for them at all. In her final half hour she was repeatedly screaming someone's name over and over again."

This begins to make me tear up, I have a feeling I know the name she was screaming. I need to hear the old man say the name that came from her lips. I ask him, "What was the name that she was screaming?"

He tells me, exactly as I expected…my name. I can't control my feelings any longer and I fall to the ground, crying like a man who has lost everything. I have so much mental anguish piercing through my mind as I learn she was screaming for me as she was being tortured. I am dying inside because I feel like I have let her down.

I start screaming, "How can I ever forgive myself? How can I continue to live with the knowledge that I failed her, I can't even respect myself now. At this moment I feel like I am the biggest coward alive."

The old man taps me on the back and says in a soothing voice, "I am sorry son, but I told you sometimes stories are better off untold."

Afraid that he won't continue, I wipe my tears and stand before him as a strong man. "Please continue, don't stop now," I beg.

"There is nothing left to say," the old man answers.

I look him in the eyes asking, "If there is anything else, please don't hesitate to tell me."

He shrugs his shoulders saying, "There was one final earth shattering scream and then all was silent from within the house. If you don't mind my asking, how did they kill her?"

I am taken back by his question, unprepared to answer. Pausing for a few moments, wondering if I want him to know, I remember that he has seen the worst. He had his entire family slaughtered in front of his own eyes. This reinforced the thought that he had earned the right to know on top of the fact that he informed me of the missing time line before her death.

Breaking the silence, I tell him, "They tortured her body so badly that some parts of her body were missing." Not giving him the painful details. "In the end they opened her from inside her southern opening to her navel with a sharp object."

The old man takes a deep breath to prevent him from losing control of his emotions and says, "I have known Rola since she was born. I watched her grow up in our back yards. She was a dear friend to my eldest granddaughter. She would play and eat at our house quite often. I loved her in the same manner as I loved my own granddaughter. However, they are all gone now, and there is no bringing them back. All we can do is ask God to give us the patience and strength to carry on. Believe me my boy…God has a reason for everything that happens to us. What ever his reason is to why this occurred, it is okay with me."

Placing his hand on my shoulder, he says "Let me give you some advice." Opening his hands to the heaven and leaning his head back to stare above, "Never question God's will. Thank you God for everything, good or bad. Son, you should do the same," he says as he looks into my eyes. "Don't let what happened here

make you lose your faith, those butchers and who ever else is behind them want us to lose our faith. They know that we are strong because of our faith. Remember one thing, God gives, and God takes. Don't ever forget that. Only faith will give you the strength and the power to move beyond this hard time."

Opening his hands again, palms toward the heavens, he says, "Come on, you and I together, let's ask God to take our loved ones and all who suffered and died in this massacre to the heavens. For those who hadn't cleansed their souls, may God forgive and have mercy on them."

I listen to him until he says, "May God forgive those killers and show them the right path for forgiveness," this make me terribly upset. I do not believe what he just said.

"Are you asking God to forgive those butchers?!" I yell.

He sighs and says, "Son, don't be so hateful like them. Wish for your enemy what you would wish for yourself. This is how you will make peace with God as well as your enemy."

I find his speech beautiful. There is no question in my mind that this old man gave me peace within my heart as well as with God.

He gives me a warm smile and asks, "May I leave now? I came here for some sugar and by now my tea is cold. I believe I won't need the sugar now. Son, think about what I have told you," he says as he walks away with the sugar jar.

I stand in the doorway thinking that what he gave me was worth more then a jar of sugar. He gave me peace of mind when it comes to my feelings of betrayal with Rola's death, as well as peace of mind regarding how I can soldier on with my own life. He has lifted a great burden off of my shoulders in the thirty minutes that we have conversed.

I turn around to take a final look at the house I once knew as a happy home. I can't help but think this house is now vacant, and no one is here to claim ownership of it. With all the homeless families living in the camps, I know this house won't stay empty for long. I decide to leave the main door open as a sign showing that this home is available for anyone who might need it.

I step onto the main street and begin walking…looking forward to a better future then the past.

THE END

Rola's final resting place in Shatila Camp

FINAL THOUGHTS

I would like to start this note by saying it truly breaks my heart to reopen a wound that was made by the massacre almost a quarter of a century ago. This wound slowly reopened the moment I decided to write this book. This true story was buried inside me until I decided to share it with the rest of the world. I felt that what had happened at the Sabra and Shatila camps in September 1982 should be told. I owe it to the victims of the massacre.

It is a true story and it is written exactly as it happened and how I personally experienced it. I know for a fact that some groups or governments will not be happy to see this story brought back to life. They have tried to bury this story along with the victims of the massacre.

My life was spared for a reason—to tell the outside world what really occurred *during* the massacre, not just the before and after. This untold story will prove to the modern societies that hate and revenge still exist among all peoples. It is suppressed until the day when it can be used as the worst weapon known to human kind.

I witnessed the destructive forces of this weapon. The hate and revenge left behind over thirty-five-hundred dead, most of them women, children and elderly men. What had driven those butchers to torture women and kill children of all ages? Is it hate or revenge or possibly both? I witnessed the murders of those unarmed and defenseless civilians on the streets of Sabra and Shatila camps.

I saw the victims' faces as they were being slaughtered by the armed forces. I could tell by the expressions on their faces that they had no idea why they were being raped and killed in the most horrific of ways. All they knew was that the P.L.O. had evacuated Beirut so that the Palestinians left behind could live in peace, not knowing that hate knows no peace—only revenge.

The people of both camps were very simple people, living under the worst conditions. They were not aware that they were surrounded by enemies. Those butchers knew that there were no P.L.O. fighters left behind in the camps. That is the reason why they infiltrated the camp to kill nearly the entire population. If they had known for a fact that there were two hundred P.L.O. fighters in the camps they would have never attempted an attack on the camps. This is the same reason that they never attacked before. Those cowards were scared of facing the P.L.O. It's a fact. So now, we know that they are not only murderers, but disgusting and brutal cowards as well.

If history tells us anything, it is that cowards always stab you in the back. They never confront you face to face. It is well known that cowards will break a promise to anyone, at any time. Which is exactly what they did when the Israelis broke the promise to the Americans regarding entering and occupying West Beirut. They entered with only one intention, produce more bloodshed. Otherwise, they had no business in Beirut, because the P.L.O. had evacuated the city. I can't think of any other reason why they would occupy Beirut except to unleash the blood thirsty butchers against the refugee camps. This is the only common factor between the Israeli soldiers and the Christian Phalangist—the thirst for more Palestinian blood.

Later I learned that the Israelis had explained to the Americans that Sabra and Shatila were an accident. I couldn't help but think that this execution of innocent civilians was simply the way they planned it. I wish I had had the opportunity to explain to Mr. Sharon what an accident is. An accident is when you step on a banana peel and slip—this is an accident. How dare he be the cause of raping and murdering over thirty-five-hundred souls? How can this be an accident when it was planned?

I know for a fact that when they raped, tortured and killed my Rola, it was no accident. It was murder. Someone needed to explain to the Hitler of Israel the difference between an accident and a murder. I will leave this explanation to the professionals. I would have liked to ask Sharon, "We have buried our dead bodies, can you bury your shame?" I know that he can not, because he has been living with it for the last quarter of a century.

I would like to send this message to the Israeli Government—I

will not forget the Sabra and Shatila massacre, but I am willing to forgive, if they are ready to look forward to a peaceful future without hate, revenge or fear. Let's give each other a chance to live together in the same country under one God so that our chldren may have a better life in a peaceful world. I am not going to say, "Death to Israel," as I realize that they have the right to live as we do.

The problem we are facing is between two rights. The question being why is it so difficult to *make* things right? Peace is the answer to all our prayers, yet we choose war. There is a very tenuous line between peace and war, and we have a choice between one or the other in every action we take. If it is a choice, then together let's use the blood of Sabra and Shatila victims as fuel to steer us towards a permanent and final peace.

God Bless,

Marco Abraham

AUTHOR'S NOTES

This is my story as you lived it with me minute by minute. You might have heard about this massacre that took place in mid-September of 1982 in both refugee camps of Sabra and Shatila in Beirut, Lebanon. As you read my book, you shared this experience with me and you know exactly how my people suffered before, during and after this massacre took place. You read about how my people were forced to eat cats, rats, dogs and finally human flesh to avoid dying from starvation. We did survive before the massacre, but not for long.

We were blamed for the assassination of the elected president of Lebanon, Bashir Gemayel just a day or two prior to the massacre. This is when the Israeli Defense Minister Ariel Sharon,

decided to use the Lebanese Christian Phalangists to slaughter the people of both camps. The Israelis saw an opportunity to kill two birds with one stone. They knew that the Christian Phalangists were hungry for revenge for the assassination of their president elect. They blamed the Palestinians for his death. Later, it was determined that the Palestinians had not been responsible for the assassination.

After his assassination, the Israeli army moved in to occupy West Beirut, breaking the promise to the Americans that they would not enter the city if the P.L.O. evacuated Beirut. This was a promise that they couldn't help but break. Right away the Israelis held a meeting with the Phalangists officers where they agreed to allow the Phalangists militiamen to hunt down the remaining P.L.O. fighters in the Sabra and Shatila camps.

A second meeting was attended by Elie Hobeika, the leader of the Lebanese Christian Phalangists. During this meeting it was agreed that he would be in charge of this operation. The massacre began that night.

The Israeli commission of inquiry into the massacre recalled how Hobeika was asked by a Phalangists colleague over the radio, "What should be done with the fifty Palestinian women and children prisoners?" He had replied, "This is the last time you are going to ask me a question like that. You know exactly what to do."

His colleague had laughed in his response. From that time on the Phalangists for the next forty-two hours non-stop raped, and killed every woman, child, and old man. In these two camps, under the eyes and ears of the Israelis. Who had the two camps under their control?

On the next day of the massacre, Morris Draper, one of President Reagan's envoys, sent a message to Sharon saying, "You must stop the massacre. This is obscene. I have an officer in the camps, counting the bodies. You ought to be ashamed. The situation is rotten and terrible. They are killing children. You were in absolute control of the area, and therefore responsible for the area."

That was Morris Draper's exact words to the Israeli's defense minister Ariel Sharon. Neither Hobeika nor Ariel Sharon ever accepted responsibility of this massacre. So the blood of the victims of Sabra and Shatila Massacre will remain lost.

When the scale of the massacre became known and photographs of the bodies in the refugee camps began to be published in the world press, Israel was held directly responsible for the atrocity. The Israeli public was shocked. On September 25th, a huge demonstration of 300,000 Israelis was held in Tel Aviv demanding the resignation of Prime Minister Menahem Begin and Defense Minister Ariel Sharon and that a judicial commission of inquiry to investigate the massacre be established.

A commission was appointed to investigate, headed by Supreme Court President Yitzhak Kahan. Its members included Supreme Court Justice Aharon Barak and Major General (Res.) Yona Efrat. The Kahan Commission issued its report on February 8th, 1983. With regard to Sharon, the panel recommended that he:

> ...draw the appropriate personal conclusions arising out of the defects revealed with regard to the manner in which he discharged the duties of his office."

In other words, that he resign or if necessary, that the prime minister exercise his authority to remove the defense minister from office.

The key paragraphs relating to Sharon's responsibilities were these:

- In our view, the minister of defense made a grave mistake when he ignored the danger of acts of revenge and bloodshed by the Phalangists against the population in the refugee camps ... it is our view that responsibility is to be imputed to the minister of defense for having disregarded the danger of acts of vengeance and bloodshed by the Phalangists against the population of the refugee camps, and having failed to take this danger into account when he decided to move the Phalangists into the camps.
- In addition, responsibility is to be imputed to the minister of defense for not ordering appropriate measures for preventing or reducing the danger of massacre as a condition for the Phalangists' entry into the camps. These blunders constitute the non-fulfillment of a duty with which the defense minister was charged.

Former US Secretary of State Henry Kissinger said of the Kahan Commission:

- [It was] a great tribute to Israeli democracy...there are very few governments in the world that one can imagine making such a public investigation of such a difficult and shameful episode

* * * * *

In 2001, Palestinian survivors of the massacre demanded that the prime minister Ariel Sharon be indicted on War Crime charges in Belgium under a 1993 Belgium law that allows this type of complaint to be filled by non-nationals.

* * * * *

Elie Hobeika, the leader of the Lebanese Christian Phalangists, was killed in a massive bomb attack at his house in the Beirut Suburb of Hazmiyeh. His death at the age of forty-five came at a time when he had agreed to testify against Israeli prime minister Ariel Sharon in a War Crimes trial that may be held later in a Brussels court.

TESTIMONIES

A description of the scene as given by Loren Jenkins of the Washington Post service on September 23, 1982:

"The scene at the Shatila camp when foreign observers entered Saturday morning was like a nightmare. Women wailed over the deaths of loved ones, bodies began to swell under the hot sun, and the streets were littered with thousands of spent cartridges. Houses had been dynamited and bulldozed into rubble, many with the inhabitants still inside. Groups of bodies lay before bullet-pocked walls where they appeared to have been executed. Others were strewn in alleys and streets, apparently shot as they tried to escape. Each little dirt alley through the deserted buildings, where

Palestinians have lived since fleeing Palestine when Zionists raped Palestine in 1948, told its own horror story.

In one, 16 men lay piled on top of each other, frozen into grotesque, contorted positions. Nearby, on a small, simple concrete patio, a lone woman about 40 years old, wearing a gingham dress and with her head in a scarf, staring at the blue sky.

Further up the main street of the camp that leads towards the Palestinian shantytown of Sabra, other bodies lay twisted amid the rubble of buildings bulldozed out of the way. Next to a small shop, the body of 70-year-old Abu Diab Derani was crumpled against a wall, his head buried in the dirt, a hand outstretched in a surreal pose towards a lone women's shoe in the dirt. He had been shot at close range in the temple."

Excerpt from Inquiry Testimony

Ralph Schoenman and Mya Shone, two American journalists who spent six weeks in Lebanon, gave evidence before the International Commission of Inquiry. The following is an extract from their testimony:

"When we entered Sabra and Shatila on Saturday, September 18, 1982, the final day of the killing, we saw bodies everywhere. We photographed victims that had been mutilated with axes and knives. Only a few of the people we photographed had been machine-gunned. Others had their heads smashed, their eyes removed, their throats cut, skin was stripped from their bodies, limbs were severed, some people were eviscerated. The terrorists also found time to plunder Palestinian property as well as books, manuscripts and other cultural material from the Palestinian Research Center in Beirut."

The Massacre of Sabra & Shatila
By Ellen Siegel

Ellen Siegel is a Jewish American. She worked as a nurse in Beirut during the massacre in 1982 and testified before the Kahan Commission of Inquiry in Jerusalem. She is a founding member of the Jewish Committee for Israeli-Palestinian (Peace). She lives in Washington, D.C.

For many years I did solidarity work. In 1980 I returned to Beirut for a short period to work with Palestinian women who had established embroidery workshops in order to support themselves and lead as much of a productive life as possible.

The Israeli invasion of Lebanon in 1982 horrified me. American weapons were being used to maim and kill helpless Palestinian and Lebanese civilians and refugees. Israeli soldiers were preventing food, water, and much-needed medical supplies from entering West Beirut. The hurt and suffering of those in pain was unattended to; no dignity was even given to the dead.

I arrived in Beirut on September 2, 1982. The ashes were still smoldering. The invasion was over, the PLO fighters and administration had been evacuated, the Israeli forces had pulled back from the city.

I was assigned to a hospital, called "Gaza," in Sabra camp. The Sabra and Shatila camps of the UN Relief and Works Agency (UNRWA) lie side by side in West Beirut. They are two of the 12 camps established in Lebanon since 1948 by UNRWA to shelter Palestinians exiled from their homes because of the creation of Israel. Before the 1982 invasion about 90,000 people lived there, a fourth of them poor Lebanese. The houses were mainly one-story concrete dwellings with corrugated iron roofs. Camp buildings and homes were tightly packed together, separated by numerous narrow alleyways.

The camp inhabitants lived and worked together. A welfare and educational system, municipal councils, and trade unions existed. Committees organized vocational training in such areas as embroidery and carpentry and operated kindergartens. By the time I arrived in Beirut, the camps' population had shrunk to about 10,000.

The Israeli army had left behind the effects of the U.S. implements of war. Shrapnel, ammunition, rocket casings, and other such armaments, many of them "made in USA," were everywhere. Because of them, the hospitals were filled with victims of chemical burns, with dehydrated babies, with recovering amputees. Supplies were limited, conditions poor. For example, because the electrical supply was irregular, we sometimes had to hold flashlights to finish an operation.

On September 14, the newly elected president of Lebanon, Bashir Gemayel of the Phalange Party, was assassinated. The next day Israeli war planes flew over West Beirut. Machine-gun fire increased as the day went on. On September 16, Israeli planes again flew over the camps; light artillery fire continued, but it was now accompanied by heavy artillery. Thousands of refugees sought security in and around the hospital. They were panic-stricken; they screamed, "Israel! Phalange!" and made a slashing motion across their throats. That evening, I watched from the tenth floor of the hospital as flares were shot into the air, lighting up neighborhoods of the camp. Sounds of machine-gun fire followed each illumination.

On the morning of the 17th, those who had sought refuge at the hospital disappeared and all the patients who could walk fled. By

afternoon, all of the Palestinian and other Arab staff members were gone; their administrator had told them that the hospital was no longer safe for them.

The high explosives were coming so close that we had to move the remaining patients to the lower floors. Smoke poured in the windows, windows cracked, doors slammed, equipment reverberated. Everything was shaking. By evening, we heard only the sounds of machine-gun fire. Tending to the very ill was more difficult than usual; to some, the bombardment made the difference between life and death.

That evening a few severely wounded people managed to be brought to the hospital. Among them was a child of 12 who was suffering from shock, a bullet injury in his leg, and an open wound on his hand where a finger had once been; his name was Mounir. Treatment of his leg began immediately to prevent amputation. Later that evening, the International Committee of the Red Cross (ICRC) was allowed to evacuate a small number of wounded children to a hospital outside of the camp area; Mounir was chosen.

Early the next morning, all the health care workers were told that the "Lebanese Army" was downstairs and that we must assemble at the hospital entrance. The armed militia we found below were in fact not the Lebanese Army but Phalangists. (These were the military wing of the Phalange Party, a nationalist Christian party founded in the 1930's on the model of European fascist groups.) They allowed us to leave one medical student and one nurse behind in the Intensive Care Unit. They marched the rest of us down the main street of Sabra and Shatila, past dead bodies and hundreds of camp residents guarded by armed militiamen.

One woman tried to pass her baby to one of the physicians, but the militiamen stopped her. Sporadic machine-gun fire could still be heard as we marched. Bulldozers, at least one marked with a Hebrew letter, were busy: homes that had stood at the edge of the camp were now rubble. As we walked along, our captors called us names—"dirty people," "un-Christian" (because we were treating "terrorists who kill Christians"), "Communists," "Socialists."

The militiamen lined us up against a bullet-riddled wall just outside the camp. Rifles ready and aimed towards us, they paused, then filed back into the camp.

Other militiamen came and took us to a courtyard on the road to what had been a United Nations building. The courtyard was littered with Israeli products and newspapers. There they questioned us about why we had come and who had sent us. Afterwards, they marched us over to a building occupied by the Israeli Defense Force (IDF). From its roof, Israeli soldiers with binoculars were looking down on both Sabra and Shatila. Here the Lebanese turned us over to the Israelis.

Israeli soldiers drove us into West Beirut and dropped us off near the American Embassy. I went in and reported to an embassy official that "something wrong was going on in those camps." He said the man in charge was out: "Come back later."

That afternoon, many of the health care workers began searching for our patients. We found that the ICRC had eventually been able to evacuate all of them to other medical facilities around Beirut.

The next day I returned to the American Embassy and gave an accounting of what I had seen.

ABOUT THE AUTHOR

Marco Abraham was born in a refugee camp called Shatila in Beirut Lebanon. Growing up was hard, he cheated death many times before the age of eighteen. He survived a Civil War, a Massacre, and the loss of many loved ones. Living in the United States has changed his perspective on life. Through many years of education, he has unleashed the creativity in his mind, and has released that creativity into his writing. He wrote about his unfortunate adolescent years in *Lost Blood.* For several years, he debated whether or not to publish this true story for all to read, and learn from. Marco is working on a novel titled "Angel~X" to be released soon.

AUTHORS OUTLOOK ON THE FUTURE

Having personally lived through a horrifying experience, I believe as a human as well as the author of the true story *Lost Blood* that it is truly time for a sincere and lasting peace. I learned first hand how ugly wars can be and what they leave behind in terms of the suffering and death of innocent women, children and elderly men.

I have seen the power of hate and revenge and how it left behind three thousand bodies on one single street. I have witnessed the rape of children before they were crushed under military boots and do not wish a similar experience to happen to anyone at any time, not even for an enemy. I truly believe this kind of violence needs to stop as I look to a better future without hate and revenge, without wars, just peace between Muslims, Jews and Christians.

It has become my fervent desire to call for fundamentalist Muslims to stop every kind of violence against the Jews and the Christians and give peace a chance—peace is what true Islam calls for. The true Muslim knows this fact. These fundamentalists groups are giving Islam an appalling reputation. Their violent acts in Iraq are killing more innocent Muslims, both Sunni and Sheia, then any other religion. Those fundamentalists are dangerous to the Islamic religion, if not the enemy of Islam. I would like free people all over the world to know that the Islamic fundamentalist does not represent me or the other true Muslims in any way. I urge every free man and woman to learn more about true Islam before passing judgment on myself and other Muslims. By doing so, your opinion of the moderate Muslims—the vast majority of the Muslim faith, will not be influenced by the militants who are by far the minority. Please do not give those fundamentalists a chance to claim victory through fear tactics and hate mongering.

Take me as a living example; I call for peace, especially between the Israelis and the Palestinians, hoping that one day my dream will come true. It is no secret that the Israeli/Palestinian conflict is the cause of many problems in the Middle East. As Americans, if we put our effort into bringing peace to these two suffering parties, we have a greater chance of keeping peace here in America. We are involved in the Middle East conflict whether we admit it or not, whether we know it or not. It is time for all of us to push for peace as the only option. This is the only way peace will become more than just a dream, my dream, your dream—and certainly their dream.

Peace,

Marco Abraham